M. Florian

History of the Moors in Spain

M. Florian

History of the Moors in Spain

ISBN/EAN: 9783337244101

Printed in Europe, USA, Canada, Australia, Japan

Cover: Foto ©ninafisch / pixelio.de

More available books at **www.hansebooks.com**

HISTORY

OF THE

MOORS OF SPAIN

TRANSLATED FROM THE FRENCH ORIGINAL OF

M. FLORIAN.

TO WHICH IS ADDED,

A BRIEF NOTICE OF ISLAMISM.

NEW YORK:

HARPER & BROTHERS, PUBLISHERS,
329 & 331 PEARL STREET,
FRANKLIN SQUARE.

1860.

Entered, according to Act of Congress, in the year 1840 by
HARPER & BROTHERS,
In the Clerk's Office of the Southern District of New York

PUBLISHERS' ADVERTISEMENT.

WE are accustomed to look upon the followers of the Arabian Prophet as little better than barbarians, remarkable chiefly for ignorance, cruelty, and a blind and persecuting spirit of fanaticism. As it regards the character of the Mohammedans at the present day, and, indeed, their moral and intellectual condition for the last two centuries, there is no great error in this opinion. But they are a degenerated race. There has been a period of great brilliancy in their history, when they were distinguished for their love of knowledge, and the successful cultivation of science and the arts; nor is it too much to say, that to them Christian Europe is indebted for the generous impulse which led to the revival of learning in the thirteenth and fourteenth centuries. Of the various nations of the great Moslem family, none were more renowned in arts, as well as arms, than the Moorish conquerors of Spain, whose history is contained in the following pages. The French original of this work has long enjoyed a deservedly high reputation; and the translation here offered is by an American lady, whose literary taste and acquirements well qualified her for the task.

A sketch of Mohammedan history, &c., from Rev. S. Greene's Life of Mohammed, has been appended at the close of the volume, to present to the reader a comprehensive view of that very remarkable people, of whom the Moors of Spain formed so distinguished a branch.

H. & B.

New-York, October, 1840.

CONTENTS.

FIRST EPOCH.

	Page
The Origin of the Moors	19
The Arabs	21
The Birth of Mohammed	23
Religion of Mohammed	23
The Progress of Islamism	25
Victories of the Mussulmans	26
New Conquests of the Mohammedans	29
The Moors become Mussulmans	32
Condition of Spain under the Goths	33
Conquest of Spain by the Moors	35
The Viceroys of Spain	36
Insurrection of Prince Pelagius	36
Abderamus attempts the Conquest of France	39
He penetrates as far as the Loire	41
The Battle of Tours	42
Civil Wars distract Spain	43

SECOND EPOCH.

	Page
The Kings of Cordova become the Caliphs of the West	45
The Asiatic Mussulmans divide	46
The Dynasty of the Ommiades lose the Caliphate	48
Horrible Massacre of the Ommiades	52
An Ommiade Prince repairs to Spain	53
Abderamus, the first Caliph of the West	53

CONTENTS.

Reign of Abderamus I. 54
Religion and Fêtes of the Moors of Spain 55
Civil Wars arise among the Moors 57
The Reigns of Hacchem I. and of Abdelazis . . . 58
Reign of Abderamus II. 59
Condition of the Fine Arts at Cordova . . . 60
Anecdote of Abderamus 61
Reigns of Mohammed, Almouzir, and Abdalla . . . 62
Reign of Abderamus III. 62
Embassy from a Greek Emperor 64
Magnificence and Gallantry of the Moors 64
Description of the City and Palace of Zahra . . . 65
Wealth of the Caliphs of Cordova 68
The Fine Arts cultivated at Cordova 71
Reign of El Hacchem 74
Laws of the Moors, and their Mode of administering Justice 75
Authority possessed by Fathers and old Men . . . 77
An Illustration of the Magnanimity of El Hakkam . . 78
Reign of Hacchem III. 80
Successful Rule of Mohammed Almonzir as Hadjeb under the imbecile Hacchem 80
Disorders at Cordova 82
End of the Caliphate 83

THIRD EPOCH.

The principal Kingdoms erected from the Ruins of the Caliphate of the West 85
Condition of Christian Spain at this Juncture . . . 86
The Kingdom of Toledo; its Termination . . 87, 88
Success of the Christians 89
The Cid 89
The Kingdom of Seville 91
The Dynasty of the Almoravides hold Supremacy in Africa 92

CONTENTS ix

	Page
Conquests of the Almoravides in Spain	93
French Princes repair to Spain	94
Extinction of the Kingdom of Saragossa	95
Foundation of the Kingdom of Portugal	95
State of the Fine Arts among the Moors at this Period	97
Abenzoar and Averroes	97
Dissensions between the Moors and Christians	98
The Africans, under Mohammed *the Green*, land in Spain	100
Battle of Toloza	102–104
Tactics of the Moors	105
The discomfited Mohammed returns to Africa	109
Extent of the Territories still retained by the Moors in Spain	110
St. Ferdinand and Jaques I.	111
Valencia is attacked by the Aragonians	113
Siege of Cordova	114
Surrender of Valencia	116

FOURTH EPOCH.

	Page
The Kings of Grenada	118
The Condition of the Moors; their Despondency	118
Mohammed Alhamar; his Character and Influence with his Countrymen	119
He founds the Kingdom of Grenada	120
Description of the City of Grenada and its *Vega*	121
Extent and Resources of this Kingdom	123
Reign of Mohammed Alhamar I.	124
The Moorish Sovereign becomes the Vassal of the King of Castile	124
Ferdinand III. besieges Seville	125
The Taking of Seville	126
Revenues of the Kings of Grenada	127
Military Forces	129
Cavalry of the Moors	129

CONTENTS.

	Page
Disturbances in Castile	133
Reign of Mohammed II. El Fakik	133
He forms a League with the King of Morocco	134
Misfortunes of Alphonso of Castile	134
Interview between Alphonso and the Sovereign of Morocco	134
State of Learning and the Fine Arts under Mohammed al Mumenim	136
Description of the Alhambra	137
The Court of Lions	140
The Generalif	145
Mohammed III. El Hama, or *the Blind*, ascends the Throne of Grenada	147
Troubles in Grenada	149
Reign of Mohammed IV. Abenazar	149
Reign of Ismael	149
Reign of Mohammed V. and of Joseph I.	152
The Battle of Salado	152
Successive Reigns of Mohammed VI. and Mohammed VII.	154
Horrible Crime of Peter the Cruel of Castile	156
Condition of Spain—of Europe in general	156, 157
Mohammed VI. reassumes the Crown	158
Reign of Mohammed VIII. Abouhadjad	158
Favourite Literary and Scientific Pursuits of the Moors under the munificent Rule of Abouhadjad	160
Universal prevalence of a Taste for Fiction among the Arabs	161
Music and Gallantry of the Moors	162
The mixture of Refinement and Ferocity in the Character of the Moors	166
Description of the Women of Grenada	169
The national Costume of both Sexes	170
Moorish Customs	171
Folly of the Grand-master of Alcantara	172
The Result of his Expedition	174
Dreadful Death of Joseph II.	175
Mohammed IX. usurps the Throne	175
Singular Escape of a condemned Prince	176

CONTENTS.

	Page
Generous Disposition of Joseph III.	176
Disturbed Condition of the Kingdom after his Death	177
A rapid Succession of Rulers	177, 178
Reign of Ismael II.	178
The Miseries of War most severely felt by the Cultivator of the Soil	179
Mulei Hassem succeeds Ismael II.	179
Marriage of Ferdinand and Isabella	180
The respective Characters of these Sovereigns	181
They declare War against the Grenadians	182
Statesmen and Soldiers of the Spanish Court	182
Stern Reply of the Grenadian King	183
Alhama is Surprised	184
Civil War is kindled in Grenada by the Feuds of the Royal Family	184
Boabdil is proclaimed King	185
Cause of the ambitious hopes of Zagal	185
Boabdil is taken Prisoner by the Spaniards	186
The politic Spanish Rulers restore Boabdil to Liberty	187
The Moors become their own Destroyers	187
Death of Mulei-Hassem	187
Boabdil and his Uncle divide the Relics of Grenada between them	188
Baseness of Zagal	188
Boabdil reigns alone at Grenada	188
Ferdinand lays Siege to the City of Grenada	189
Condition of the City	189
The Spanish Camp	191
Isabella repairs to the Camp	191
She builds a City	192
Surrender of Grenada	194
Departure of Boabdil from the City	194
The entrance of the Spanish Conquerors into the City	195
Summary of the Causes of the Ruin of the Moors	196
Characteristics of the Moors	197

	Page
Anecdote illustrative of their Observance of the Laws of Hospitality	198
Christian Persecution of the Moors	199
Revolts of the Moors, and their Results	199
Final Expulsion of the Moors from Spain	201
Notes	203

INTRODUCTION.

The name of the Moors of Spain recalls recollections of gallantry and refinement, and of the triumphs of arts and arms. But, though thus celebrated, not much is generally known of the history of that remarkable people.

The fragments of their annals, scattered among the writings of the Spanish and Arabian authors, furnish little else than accounts of murdered kings, national dissensions, civil wars, and unceasing contests with their neighbours. Yet, mingled with these melancholy recitals, individual instances of goodness, justice, and magnanimity occasionally present themselves. These traits, too, strike us more forcibly than those of a similar description with which we meet in perusing the histories of other nations; perhaps in consequence of the peculiar colouring of originality lent them by their Oriental characteristics; or perhaps because, in contrast with numerous examples of barbarity, a noble action, an eloquent discourse, or a touching expression, acquire an unusual charm.

It is not my intention to write the history of the Moors in minute detail, but merely to retrace their principal revolutions, and attempt a faithful sketch of their national character and manners.

The Spanish historians, whom I have carefully consulted in aid of this design, have been of but little assistance to me in my efforts. Careful to give a very prominent place in their extremely complicated narratives to the various sovereigns of Asturia, Navarre, Aragon, and Castile, they advert to the Moors only when their wars with the Christians inseparably mingle the interests of the two nations; but they never allude to the government, customs, or laws of the enemies of their faith.

INTRODUCTION.

The translations from the Arabian writers to which I have had recourse, throw little more light upon the subject of my researches than the productions of Spanish authors. Blinded by fanaticism and national pride, they expatiate with complacency on the warlike achievements of their countrymen, without even adverting to the reverses that attended their arms, and pass over whole dynasties without the slightest notice or comment.

Some of our *savans* have, in several very estimable works, united the information to be collected from these Spanish and Arabian histories, with such additional particulars as they were able to derive from their own personal observations.

I have drawn materials from all these sources, and have, in addition, sought for descriptions of the manners of the Moors in the Spanish and ancient Castilian romances, and in manuscripts and memoirs obtained from Madrid.

It is after these long and laborious researches

that I venture to offer a brief history of a people who bore so little resemblance to any other; who had their national vices and virtues, as well as their characteristic physiognomy; and who so long united the bravery, generosity, and chivalry of the Europeans, with the excitable temperament and strong passions of the Orientals.

To render the order of time more intelligible, and the more clearly to elucidate facts, this historical sketch will be divided in four principal Epochs.

The *first* will extend from the commencement of the Conquests of the Arabs to the Establishment of the Dynasty of the Ommiade princes at Cordova: the *second* will include the reigns of the Caliphs of the West: in the *third* will be related all that can now be ascertained concerning the various small kingdoms erected from the ruins of the Caliphate of Cordova: and the *fourth* will comprehend a narration of the prominent events in the lives of the successive sovereigns of the Kingdom of Grenada, until the peri-

INTRODUCTION. xvii

od of the final expulsion of the Mussulmans from that country.

Care has been taken to compare the dates according to the Mohammedan method of computing time, with the periods fixed by the ordinary mode of arrangement. Some of the Spanish historians, Garabai for instance, do not agree with the Arabian chronologists in relation to the years of the Hegira. I have thought proper to follow the Arabian authorities, and have adopted, with occasional corrections, the chronological arrangements of M. Cardonne, whose personal assurance I possess, that he attaches high importance to his calculations on this subject. I have thus reason to hope that this little work will serve to elucidate many points hitherto doubtful in relation to this matter.

The proper names of the Moors vary even more in the different authorities than their statements respecting the date of events, either in consequence of the difficulty of pronouncing them, or from ignorance of their proper orthography. In instances of this character I have always given the preference to such as appeared to be most generally adopted, and were, at the same time, most harmonious in sound.

A HISTORY

OF THE

MOORS OF SPAIN.

FIRST EPOCH.

THE CONQUESTS OF THE ARABS OR MOORS.

Extending from the end of the Sixth Century to the middle of the Eighth.

THE primitive Moors were the inhabitants of the vast portion of Africa bounded on the east by Egypt, on the north by the Mediterranean, on the west by the Atlantic, and on the south by the deserts of Barbary.

The origin of the Moors, or Mauritanians, is, like that of most other ancient nations, obscure, and the information we possess concerning their early history confusedly mingled with fables. The fact, however, appears to be established, that Asiatic emigrations were, from the earliest times, made into Africa. In addition to this, the historians of remote ages speak of a certain Meleck Yarfrick, king of Arabia Felix, who conducted a people called *Sabæi** into Libya, made himself master of that country, established his followers there, and gave it the name of Africa. It is from these Sabians or *Sabæi* that the principal Moorish tribes pretend to trace their descent. The derivation of the name Moors† is also supposed, in some degree, to confirm the impression that they came originally from Asia.

But, without enlarging upon these ancient statements, let it suffice to say, that nearly certain ground exists for the belief that the original Moors were Arabians. In confirmation of this impression, we find that, during every period of the existence of their race, the descendants of the primitive inhabitants of Mauritania have, like the Arabs, been divided into distinct tribes, and, like them, have pursued a wild and wandering mode of existence.

The Moors of Africa are known in ancient

---

* The *Sabæi*, according to the best ancient authorities, were the inhabitants of the extensive Arabian kingdom of Saba.—*Translator.*

† The term Moors, according to Bochart, comes from a Hebrew word, *Mahuran*, which signifies Western.

history under the name of Nomades, Numidæ or Numidians, Getulæ, and Massyli. They were by turns the subjects, the enemies, or the allies of the Carthaginians, and with them they fell under the dominion of the Romans.

After several unsuccessful revolts, to which they were instigated by their fiery, restless, and inconstant temper, the Moors were at length subjugated by the Vandals, A.D. 427.

A century afterward these people were conquered by Belisarius: but the Greeks were in their turn subdued by the Arabs, who then proceeded to achieve the conquest of Mauritania.

As, from the period when that event occurred, the Mauritanians or Moors, who were thus suddenly converted to Mohammedanism, have frequently been confounded with the *native Arabians*, it will be proper to say a few words concerning that extraordinary people: a people who, after occupying for so many centuries an insignificant place among the nations of the earth, rapidly rendered themselves masters of the greater part of the known world.

The Arabs are, beyond question, one of the most ancient races of men in existence;* and

* It is scarcely necessary to remind the reader that these

have, of all others, perhaps, best preserved their national independence, and their distinctive character and manners. Divided from the most remote times into tribes that either wandered in the desert or were collected together in cities, and obedient to chiefs who in the same person united the warrior and the magistrate, they have never been subjected to foreign domination. The Persians, the Romans, and the Macedonians vainly attempted to subdue them: they only shattered their weapons in fragments against the rocks of the Nabatheans.* Proud of an origin which he traced back even to the patriarchs of olden time, exulting in his successful defence of his liberty and his rights, the Arab, from the midst of his deserts, regarded the rest of mankind as consisting of mere bands of slaves, changing masters as chance or conve-

Children of the Desert are supposed to be the lineal descendants of Ishmael, the wandering, outcast son of the patriarch Abraham and the much-abused Hagar.—*Translator.*

* The primitive name of the Arabs, from *Nabathæa*, an appellation for their country which is probably derived from *Nabath*, the son of Ishmael. The capital city of Nabathæa was that *Petra*, of whose present appearance and condition our eminent countryman, Stephens, has given his readers so graphic a sketch in his " Travels," &c.—*Translator.*

nience directed. Brave, temperate, and indefatigable, inured from infancy to the severest toil, fearing neither thirst, hunger, nor death itself—these were a people by whose assistance a leader suitably endowed could render himself master of the world. Mohammed appeared:* to him nature had accorded the requisite qualifications for executing such a design. Courageous, sagacious, eloquent, polished, possessed in an eminent degree of the powers which both awe and delight mankind, Mohammed would have been a great man had he belonged to the most enlightened age—among an ignorant and fanatical people he became a prophet.

Until Mohammed arose among them, the Arab tribes, surrounded by Jews, Christians, and idolators, had entertained a superstitious faith, compounded of the religious belief of their various neighbours and that of the ancient Sabæi They fully credited the existence of genii, demons, and witchcraft, adored the stars, and offered idolatrous sacrifices. But Mohammed—after having devoted many years to profound and solitary meditation upon the new dogmas he designed to establish; after having either convinced

* A.D. 569.

or won to his interests the principal individuals of his own family,* possessing pre-eminent consequence among their countrymen—suddenly began to preach a new religion, opposed to all those with which the Arabs were hitherto familiar, and whose principles were well-adapted to inflame the ardent temper of that excitable people.

Children of Ishmael, said the Prophet to them, I bring you the faith that was professed by your father Abraham, by Noah, and by all the patriarchs. There is but one God, the Sovereign Ruler of all worlds: he is called THE MERCIFUL; worship Him alone. Be beneficent towards orphans, slaves, captives, and the poor: be just to all men—justice is the sister of piety. Pray and bestow alms. You will be rewarded in Heaven, by being permitted to dwell perpetually in delicious gardens, where limpid waters will for ever flow, and where each one of you will eternally enjoy the companionship of women who will be ever beautiful, ever youthful, ever devoted to you alone. Courageously combat both the unbelieving and the impious. Oppose them until they

* The Coheshirites, the guardians of the Temple of the Caaba at Mecca.

embrace Islamism* or render you tribute. Every soldier who dies in battle will share the treasures of God; nor can the coward prolong his life; for the moment when he is destined to be smitten by the angel of death is written in the Book of the Eternal.

Such precepts, announced in majestic and highly figurative language, embellished with the charms of verse, and presented by a warrior, prophet, poet, and legislator, professing to be the representative of an angel, to the most susceptible people in the world—to a people possessing a passion alike for the marvellous and the voluptuous, for heroism and for poetry—could scarcely fail to find disciples. Converts rapidly crowded around Mohammed, and their numbers were soon augmented by persecution His enemies obliged the Prophet to fly from his native Mecca and take refuge in Medina. This flight was the epoch of his glory and of the Hegira of the Mussulmans. It occurred A.D. 622.

From this moment Islamism spread like a torrent over the Arabias and Ethiopia. In vain did the Jewish and idolatrous tribes attempt to maintain their ancient faith; in vain did Mecca

* See Note A, page 203.

arm her soldiers against the destroyers of her gods; Mohammed, sword in hand, dispersed their armies, seized upon their cities, and won the affections of the people whom he subdued, by his clemency, his genius, and his fascinating address.

A legislator, a pontiff, the chief of all the Arab tribes, the commander of an invincible army, respected by the Asiatic sovereigns, adored by a powerful nation, and surrounded by captains who had become heroes in serving under him, Mohammed was on the point of marching against Heraclius, when his designs were for ever interrupted by the termination of his existence. This event took place at Medina, A.D. 632, Hegira 2, and was the effect of poison, which had, some time before, been administered to this extraordinary man by a Jewess of Rhaibar.

The death of the Prophet arrested neither the progress of his religion nor the triumphs of the Moslem arms.

Abubeker, the father-in-law of Mohammed, became his successor, and assumed the title of *Caliph*, which simply signifies *vicar*. During his reign the Saracens penetrated into Syria, dispersed the armies of Heraclius, and took the city of Damascus, the siege of which will be for ever celebrated in consequence of the almost superhuman exploits of the famous Kaled, surnamed the *Sword of God.**

Notwithstanding these successive victories, and the enormous amount of booty thus taken from the enemy and committed to his keeping, Abubeker appropriated to his own particular use a sum scarcely equivalent to forty cents a day.

Omar, the successor of Abubeker, commanded Kaled to march against Jerusalem. That city soon became the prize of the Arabs; Syria and Palestine were subdued; the Turks and the Persians demanded peace; Heraclius fled from Antioch; and all Asia trembled before Omar and the terrible Mussulmans.

Modest, in spite of the triumphs that everywhere attended them, and attributing their success to God alone, these Moslems preserved unaltered their austere manners, their frugality, their severe discipline, and their reverence for poverty, though surrounded by the most corrupt of the nations of the earth, and exposed to the seductive influences of the delicious climates and the luxurious pleasures of some of the richest and most beau-

* See Note B, page 206.

tiful countries in the world. During the sacking of a city, the most eager and impetuous soldier would be instantly arrested in the work of pillage by the word of his chief, and would, with the strictest fidelity, deliver up the booty he had obtained, that it might be deposited in the general treasury. Even the most independent and magnificent of the heroic chiefs would hasten, in accordance with the directions of the caliph, to take the command of an army, and would become successively generals, private soldiers, or ambassadors, in obedience to his slightest wish. In fine, Omar himself—Omar, the richest, the greatest, the most puissant of the monarchs of Asia, set forward upon a journey to Jerusalem, mounted upon a red camel, which bore a sack of barley, one of rice, a well-filled water-skin, and a wooden vase. Thus equipped, the caliph travelled through the midst of conquered nations, who crowded around his path at every step, entreating his blessing and praying him to adjudge their quarrels. At last he joined his army, and, inculcating precepts of simplicity, valour, and humility upon the soldiers, he made his entrance into the Holy City, liberated such of its former Christian possessors as had become the captives of his people, and commanded the preservation of the churches. Then remounting his camel, the representative of the Prophet returned to Medina, to perform the duties of the high-priest of his religion.

The Mussulmans now advanced towards Egypt. That country was soon subdued. Alexandrea was taken by Amrou, one of the most distinguished generals of Omar. It was then that the famous library was destroyed, whose loss still excites the profound regrets of the learned. The Arabians, though such enthusiastic admirers of their national poetry, despised the literature of all the rest of the world. Amrou caused the library of the Ptolemies to be burned, yet this same Amrou was nevertheless celebrated for his poetical effusions. He entertained the sincerest affection and respect for the celebrated John the Grammarian, to whom, but for the opposing order of the caliph, he would have given this valuable collection of books. It was Amrou, too, who caused the execution of a design worthy of the best age of Rome, that of connecting the Red Sea with the Mediterranean by means of a navigable canal, at a point where the waters of the Nile might be diverted from their course for its supply. This canal, so useful to Egypt, and so important to the commerce of both Europe and Asia, was accomplished in a few months. The Turks, in more modern times, have suffered it to be destroyed.

Amrou continued to advance into Africa, while the other Arabian commanders passed the Euphrates and conquered the Persians. But Omar was already no more, and Othman occupied his place.

It was during the reign of this caliph that the Saracens, banishing for ever its enfeebled Greek masters, conquered Mauritania, or the country of the Moors of Africa, A.D. 647, Heg. 27.

The invaders met with serious resistance only from the warlike tribes of the Bereberes.* That bold and pastoral people, the descendants of the ancient inhabitants of Numidia, and preserving, even to this day, a species of independence, intrenched as they are in the Atlas Mountains, long and successfully resisted the conquerors of the Moors. A Moslem general named Akba finally succeeded in subjugating them, and in compelling them to adopt the laws and faith of his country.

* See note C, page 207.

After that achievement Akba carried his arms to the extreme western point of Africa, the ocean alone resisting him in his progress. There, inspired by courage and devotion with feelings of the highest enthusiasm, he forced his horse into the waves, and, drawing his sabre, cried, " God of Mohammed, thou beholdest that, but for the element which arrests me, I would have proceeded in search of unknown nations, whom I would have forced to adore thy name!"

Until this epoch, the Moors, under the successive dominion of the Carthaginians, the Romans, the Vandals, and the Greeks, had taken but little interest in the affairs of their different masters.

Wandering in the deserts, they occupied themselves chiefly with the care of their flocks; paid the arbitrary imposts levied upon them, sometimes passively enduring the oppression of their rulers, and sometimes essaying to break their chains; taking refuge, after each defeat of their efforts, in the Atlas Mountains, or in the interior of their country.

Their religion was a mixture of Christianity and idolatry; their manners those of the enslaved Nomades: rude, ignorant, and wretched, their condition was the prototype of what it now is under the tyrants of Morocco.

But the presence of the Arabs rapidly produced a great change among these people. A common origin with that of their new masters, together with similarity of language and temperament, contributed to bind the conquered to their conquerors.

The announcement of a religion which had been preached by a descendant of Ishmael, whom the Moors regarded as their father; the rapid conquests of the Mussulmans, who were already masters of half of Asia and a large portion of Africa, and who threatened to enslave the world, aroused the excitable imaginations of the Moors, and restored to their national character all its passionate energy. They embraced the dogmas of Mohammed with transport; they united with the Arabs, volunteered to serve under the Moslem banners, and suddenly became simultaneously enamoured with Islamism and with glory.

This reunion, which doubled the military strength of the two united nations, was disturbed for some time by the revolt of the Bereberes, who never yielded their liberty under any circumstances.

The reigning caliph, Valid the First, despatched into Egypt Moussa-ben-Nazir, a judicious and valiant commander, at the head of a hundred thousand men, A.D. 708, Heg. 89.

Moussa defeated the Bereberes, restored quiet in Mauritania, and seized upon Tangier, which belonged to the Goths of Spain.

Master of an immense region of country, of a redoubtable army, and of a people who considered his supremacy as essential to their wellbeing, the Saracen general from this period contemplated carrying his arms into Spain.

That beautiful kingdom, after having been successively under the yoke of the Carthaginians and the Romans, had finally become the prey of the Barbarians. The Alains, the Suevi, and the Vandals had divided its provinces among them; but Euric, one of the Visigoths, who entered the country from the south of Gaul, had, towards the end of the fifth century, gained possession of the whole of Spain, and transmitted it to his descendants.

The softness of the climate, together with the effects of wealth and luxury, gradually enfeebled these conquerors, creating vices from which they had been previously free, and depriving them of the warlike qualities to which alone they had been indebted for their success. Of the kings who succeeded Euric, some were Arians and others Catholics, who abandoned their authority to the control of bishops, and occupied a throne shaken to its centre by internal disturbances. Roderick, the last of these Gothic sovereigns, polluted the throne by his vices; and both history and tradition accuse him of the basest crimes. Indeed, in the instance of nearly all these tyrants, their vices either directly occasioned, or were made the pretext of their final ruin.

The fact is well established, that Count Julian and his brother Oppas, archbishop of Toledo, both of them distinguished and influential men, favoured the irruption of the Moors into Spain.

Tarik, one of the most renowned captains of his time,* was sent into Spain by Moussa. He had at first but few troops; but he was not by this prevented from defeating the large army that, by command of Roderick, the last Gothic king, opposed his course.

Subsequently, having received re-enforcements

* See note D, page 208.

from Africa, Tarik vanquished Roderick himself at the battle of Xeres, where that unfortunate monarch perished during the general flight in which the conflict terminated, A.D. 714, Heg. 96.

After this battle, the Mohammedan general, profiting by his victory, penetrated into Estremadura, Andalusia, and the two Castiles, and took possession of the city of Toledo. Being soon after joined by Moussa, whose jealousy of the glory his lieutenant was so rapidly acquiring prompted him to hasten to his side, these two remarkable commanders, dividing their troops into several corps, achieved, in a few months, the conquest of the whole of Spain.

It should be observed, that these Moors, whom several historians have represented as bloodthirsty barbarians, did not deprive the people whom they had subjugated either of their faith, their churches, or the administrators of their laws. They exacted from the Spaniards only the tribute they had been accustomed to pay their kings. One cannot but question the existence of the ferocity that is ascribed to them, when it is remembered that the greater part of the Spanish cities submitted to the invaders without making the least attempt at resistance; that the Christians readily united themselves with the Moors; that the inhabitants of Toledo desired to assume the name of *Musarabs;* and that Queen Egilona, the widow of Roderick, the last of the Gothic sovereigns, publicly espoused, with the united consent of the two nations, Abdelazis the son of Moussa.

Moussa, whom the success of Tarik had greatly exasperated, wishing to remove a lieutenant whose achievements eclipsed his own, preferred an accusation against him to the caliph. Valid recalled them both, but refused to adjudge their difference, and suffered them to die at court from chagrin at seeing themselves forgotten.

Abdelazis, the husband of Egilona, became governor of Spain A.D. 718, Heg. 100, but did not long survive his elevation. Alahor, who succeeded him, carried his arms into Gaul, subdued the Warbonnais, and was preparing to push his conquests still farther, when he learned that Pelagius, a prince of the blood-royal of the Visigoths, had taken refuge in the mountains of Asturia with a handful of devoted followers; that with them he dared to brave the conquerors of Spain, and had formed the bold design of attempting to rid himself of their yoke. Alahor sent some troops against him. Pelagius, intrenched with his little army in the mountain gorges, twice gave battle to the Mussulmans, seized upon several castles, and, reanimating the spirits of the Christians, whose courage had been almost extinguished by so long a succession of reverses, taught the astonished Spaniards that the Moors were not invincible.

The insurrection of Pelagius occasioned the recall of Alahor by the Caliph Omar II. Elzemah, his successor, was of opinion that the most certain means of repressing revolts among a people is to render them prosperous and contented. He therefore devoted himself to the wise and humane government of Spain; to the regulation of imposts, until then quite arbitrary; and to quieting the discontents of the soldiery, and establishing their pay at a fixed rate. A lover of the fine arts, which the Arabs began from that time to cultivate, Elzemah embellished Cordova, which was his capital, and attracted thither the *savans* of the age. He was himself the author of a book containing a description of the cities, rivers, provinces, and ports of Spain; of the metals, mines, and quarries it possesses; and, in short, of almost every object of interest either in science or government.

But little disturbed by the insurrectionary movements of Pelagius, whose power was confined to the possession of some inaccessible mountain fortresses, Elzemah did not attempt to force him from his strongholds, but, impelled by the ardent desire of extending the Moorish conquests into France, with which the governors of Spain were ever inflamed, he passed the Pyrenees, and perished in a battle fought against Eudes, duke of Aquitania, A.D. 722, Heg. 104.

During the remainder of the Caliphate of Yezid II.,* several governors followed each other in rapid succession after the death of Elzemah.† None of their actions merit recital; but, during this period, the brave Pelagius aggrandized his petty state, advancing into the mountains of Leon, and, in addition, making himself master of several towns.

This hero, whose invincible daring roused the Asturians and Cantabrians to struggle for liberty, laid the foundations of that powerful monarchy

---

* See Note E, page 208.

† Ambeza, Azra, Jahiah, Osman, Hazifa, Hacchem, and Mohammed.

whose warriors afterward pursued the Moors even to the rocks of the Atlas.

The Moslems, who dreamed only of new conquests, made no considerable efforts against Pelagius: they were confident of checking his rebellion with the utmost ease when they should have accomplished the subjugation of the French dominions; and that desire alone fired the ardent soul of the new governor Abdalrahman, or, as he is commonly called, Abderamus.

His love of glory, his valour, his genius, and, above all, his immeasurable ambition, made the Mussulman governor regard this conquest as one that could be easily effected; but he himself was destined to be the vanquished.

Charles Martel, the son of Pepin d'Heristel, and the grandfather of Charlemagne, whose exploits effaced the recollection of those of his father, and whose fame was not eclipsed by that of his grandson, was at this time mayor of the palace, under the last princes of the first race; or, rather, Charles was the real monarch of the French and German nations.

Eudes, duke of Aquitania, the possessor of Gascony and Guienne, had long maintained a quarrel with the French hero. Unable longer, without assistance, to resist his foe, he sought an alliance with a Moor named Munuza, who was the governor of Catalonia and the secret enemy of Abderamus. These two powerful vassals, both discontented with their respective sovereigns, and inspired as much by fear as dislike, united themselves in the closest bonds, in despite of the difference in their religious faith. The Christian duke did not hesitate to give his daughter in marriage to his Mohammedan ally, and the Princess Numerance espoused the Moorish Munuza, as Queen Egilona had espoused the Moorish Abdelazis.

Abderamus, when informed of this alliance, immediately divined the motives which had induced it. He soon assembled an army, penetrated with rapidity into Catalonia, and attacked Munuza, who was wounded in a fruitless endeavour to fly, and afterward perished by his own hand. His captive wife was conducted into the presence of the victorious governor Abderamus, struck with her beauty, sent the fair Numerance as a present to the Caliph Haccham, whose regard she elicited; and thus, by a singular chance, a princess of Gascony became an inmate of the seraglio of a sovereign of Damascus.

Not content with having so signally punished Munuza, Abderamus crossed the Pyrenees, traversed Navarre, entered Guienne, and besieged and took the City of Bordeaux. Eudes attempted, at the head of an army, to arrest his progress, but was repelled in a decisive engagement. Everything yielded to the Mussulman arms: Abderamus pursued his route, ravaged Perigord, Saintonge, and Poitou, appeared in triumph in Touraine, and paused only when within view of the streaming ensigns of Charles Martel.

Charles came to this rencounter followed by the forces of France, Asturia, and Bourgogne, and attended by the veteran warriors whom he was accustomed to lead to victory. The Duke of Aquitania was also in the camp. Charles forgot his private injuries in the contemplation of the common danger: this danger was pressing: the fate of France and Germany—indeed, of the whole of Christendom, depended on the event of the approaching conflict.

Abderamus was a rival worthy of the son of Pepin. Flushed, like him, with the proud recollection of numerous victories; at the head of an innumerable army; surrounded by experienced captains, who had been the frequent witnesses of his martial triumphs; and long inspired with the warmest hopes of finally adding to the dominion of Islamism the only country belonging to the ancient Roman empire that still remained unsubdued by the Saracens, the Moorish leader met his brave foe, upon equal terms, on the battle-field of Tours, A.D. 733, Heg. 114.

The action was long and bloody. Abderamus was slain ; and this dispiriting loss, without doubt, decided the defeat of his army.* Historians assert that more than three hundred thousand men perished. This statement is probably exaggerated ; but it is certainly true, that the Moors, who had thus penetrated into the midst of France, were relentlessly pursued after their defeat, and were many of them unable to escape from the arms of the victors and the vengeance of the people.

This memorable battle, of which we possess no details, saved France from the yoke of the Arabs, and effectually arrested their spreading dominion.

Once again, subsequent to this reverse, the Moors attempted to penetrate into France, and

* It was in this battle that Charles acquired the title of *Martel*, or the *Hammer*.

succeeded in seizing upon Avignon; but Charles Martel defeated them anew, retook the captured city, drove them from Narbonne, and deprived them forever of the hope with which they had so often flattered themselves.

After the death of Abderamus, Spain was torn by dissensions between the two governors* named successively by the Caliph. A third pretender arrived from Africa. A fourth added himself to the list;† factions multiplied; the different parties often had recourse to arms; chiefs were assassinated, cities taken, and provinces ravaged.

The details of these events are variously related by different historians, but possess little interest in the narrations of any.

These civil wars lasted nearly twenty years. The Christians, who had retired into Asturia, profited by them to the utmost. Alphonso I., the son-in-law and successor of Pelagius, imitated the career of that hero. He seized upon a part of Galicia and Leon, repulsed the Mussulman troops who were sent to oppose him, and rendered himself master of several towns.

The Moors, occupied by their domestic quar-

* Abdoulmelck and Akbe. † Aboulattar and Tevaba.

rels, neglected to arrest the progress of Alphonso, and from that time the growth of a miniature kingdom commenced, whose interests were inimical to those of the Saracens in Spain.

After many crimes and combats, a certain *Joseph* had succeeded in triumphing over his different rivals, and was at last reigning supreme in Cordova, when there occurred a memorable event in the East, which was destined greatly to affect the condition of Spain.

From that period, A.D. 749, Heg. 134, commences the second epoch of the empire of the Moors of Spain, which makes it necessary to revert briefly to the history of the Eastern caliphs

SECOND EPOCH.

THE KINGS OF CORDOVA BECOME THE CALIPHS OF THE WEST.

Extending from the middle of the Eighth to the commencement of the Eleventh Century.

WE have seen that, under their first three caliphs, Abubeker, Omar, and Othman, the Arabian conquerors of Syria, Persia, and Africa preserved their ancient manners, their simplicity of character, their obedience to the successors of the Prophet, and their contempt for luxury and wealth: but what people could continue to withstand the influence of such an accumulation of prosperity? These resistless conquerors turned their weapons against each other: they forgot the virtues which had rendered them invincible, and assisted by their dissensions in dismembering the empire that their valour had created.

The disastrous effects of the baneful spirit that had thus insidiously supplanted the original principles of union, moderation, and prudence, by which, as a nation, the Moslems had been actuated, were first manifested in the assassination of the Caliph Othman.

Ali, the friend, companion, and adopted son of the Prophet, whose courage, achievements, and relationship to Mohammed, as the husband of his only daughter, had rendered him so dear to the Mussulmans, was announced as the successor of Othman.

But Moavias, the governor of Syria, refused to recognise the authority of Ali, and, under the guidance of the sagacious Amrou, the conqueror of Egypt, caused himself to be proclaimed Caliph of Damascus. Upon this, the Arabians divided: those of Medina sustaining Ali, and those of Syria Moavias. The first took the name of *Alides*, the others styled themselves *Ommiades*, deriving their denomination from the grandfather of Moavias. Such was the origin of the famous schism which still separates the Turks and Persians.

Though Ali succeeded in vanquishing Moavias in the field, he did not avail himself judiciously of the advantage afforded him by his victory. He was soon after assassinated,* and the spirit and courage of his party vanished with the oc-

* See Note A, page 208.

currence of that event. The sons of Ali made efforts to reanimate the ardour of his partisans, but in vain.

Thus, in the midst of broils, revolts, and civil wars, the Ommiades still remained in possession of the Caliphate of Damascus.* It was during the reign of one of these princes, Valid the First, that the Arabian conquests extended in the East to the banks of the Ganges, and in the West to the shores of the Atlantic. The Ommiades, however, were for the most part feeble, but they were sustained by able commanders, and the an-

* The dynasty of the Ommiades, whose capital, as M. Florian informs us, was Damascus, is most familiarly known in history as that of the *Caliphs of Syria;* and the Abbassides, who succeeded them upon the throne of Islam, are usually designated as the *Caliphs of Bagdad*, which city they built, and there established the seat of their regal power and magnificence. It may be observed, in connexion with this subject, that though the authority of the Caliphs of Damascus continued to be disputed and resisted after the death of Ali, yet with that event terminated the temporary division of the civil and sacerdotal power which had been at first occasioned by their usurpation of sovereignty. The political supremacy of the party of Ali ceased with his existence, and the authority that had belonged to the immediate successors of Mohammed long continued to centre in the family of the Ommiade princes.—*Trans.*

cient valour of the Moslem soldiers was not yet degenerated.

After the Ommiades had maintained their empire for the space of ninety-three years, Mervan II.,* the last caliph of the race, was deprived of his throne and his life† through the instrumentality of Abdalla, a chief of the tribe of the Abbassides, who were, like the Ommiades, near relatives of Mohammed.

Aboul-Abbas, the nephew of Abdalla, supplanted the former caliph. With him commenced the dynasty of the Abbassides, so celebrated in the East for their love of science and their connexion with the names of Haroun Al Raschid, Almamon, and the Bermasides.‡

The Abbassides retained the caliphate during five successive centuries.§ At the termination of

* See Note B, page 209.
† A.D. 752, Heg. 134.
‡ See Note C, page 209.
§ It was under the government of the Abbassides that the empire of the East possessed that superiority in wealth, magnificence, and learning for which it was once so celebrated. Under the sway of the Caliphs of Bagdad, the Mohammedans became as much renowned for their attainments in the higher branches of science as in the elegant and useful arts. To them the civilized world is indebted for the revival of the exact and physical sciences, and the discovery or restoration

that period, they were despoiled of their power by the Tartar posterity of Gengis Khan, after of most of the arts that afterward lent such beneficial aid to the progress of European literature and refinement. The far-famed capital of the Abbassides was adorned with every attraction that the most unbounded wealth could secure, or the most consummate art perfect. There taste and power had combined exquisite luxury with unparalleled splendour, and there all that imagination could suggest to fascinate the senses or enrapture the mind, was realized. These princes of Islam, by their unbounded liberality, attracted the learning and genius of other countries to their brilliant court; several of them were the ardent lovers of science as well as the munificent patrons of its devotees. Thus Bagdad became the favoured and genial home of letters and the arts; and luxury and the pursuit of pleasure were ennobled by a graceful union with the more elevated enjoyments of cultivated intellect and refined taste. Nor were these beneficent influences confined to the Mohammedan court, or to the period of time when they were so powerfully exercised. The Moslem sovereigns gave laws to a wide realm in arts as well as arms; and if the whole of Europe did not acknowledge their political superiority, in the world of science their supremacy was everywhere undisputed. That, like the gradually enlarging circles made by a pebble thrown into calm water, continued to spread farther and farther, until it reached the most distant shores, and communicated a generous impulse to nations long sunk in intellectual night.

* * * * *

Such was the celebrated empire of the Abbassides in its halcyon days of undiminished power—such the beautiful City of having witnessed the establishment of a race of Egyptian caliphs named *Fatimites*, the pretended descendants of Fatima, the daughter of Mohammed.

Thus was the Eastern empire of the Arabs eventually destroyed: the descendants of Ishmael returned to the country from which they had originally sprung, and gradually reverted to nearly the same condition as that in which they existed when the Prophet arose among them.

Peace, the favoured home of imperial magnificence, ere the despoiling Tartar had profaned its loveliness and destroyed its grandeur. Yet, when we look beneath the brilliant exterior of these Oriental scenes and characters, we discover, under the splendour and elegance by which the eyes of the world were so long dazzled, the corruption and licentiousness of a government containing within itself the seeds of its own insecurity and ultimate destruction. We behold the absence of all fixed principles of legislation; we frequently find absolute monarchs guided solely by passion or caprice in the administration of arbitrary laws, and swaying the destinies of a people who, as a whole, were far from deriving any substantial advantage from the wealth and greatness of their despotic rulers. We are thus led to observe the evils that necessarily result from a want of those principles of vital religion, without which mere human learning is so inadequate to discipline the passions or direct the reason, and of those just and equal laws, the supremacy of which can alone secure the happiness of a people or the permanency of political institutions.—*Trans.*

These events, from the founding of the dynasty of the Abbassides, have been anticipated in point of time in the relation, because henceforth the history of Spain is no longer intermingled with that of the East.

After having dwelt briefly upon an event intimately connected as well with the establishment of the Abbassides upon the Moslem throne as with the history of Spain, we will enter continuously upon the main subject of our work.

To return, then, for a moment, to the downfall of the Ommiade caliphs.

When the cruel Abdalla had placed his nephew, Aboul-Abbas, on the throne of the Caliphs of Damascus, he formed the horrible design of exterminating the Ommiades. These princes were very numerous. With the Arabs, among whom polygamy is permitted, and where numerous offspring are regarded as the peculiar gift of Heaven, it is not unusual to find several thousand individuals belonging to the same family.

Abdalla, despairing of effecting the destruction of the race of his enemies, dispersed as they were by terror, published a general amnesty to all the Ommiades who should present themselves before him on a certain day. Those ill-fated people, confiding in the fulfilment of his solemn promises, hastened to seek safety at the feet of Abdalla. The monster, when they were all assembled, caused his soldiers to surround them, and then commanded them all to be butchered in his presence. After this frightful massacre, Abdalla ordered the bloody bodies to be ranged side by side in close order, and then to be covered with boards spread with Persian carpets. Upon this horrible table he caused a magnificent feast to be served to his officers. One shudders at the perusal of such details, but they serve to portray the character of this Oriental conqueror.

A solitary Ommiade escaped the miserable fate of his brethren; a prince named Abderamus. A fugitive wanderer, he reached Egypt, and concealed himself in the solitary recesses of its inhospitable deserts.

The Moors of Spain, faithful to the Ommiades, though their governor Joseph had recognised the authority of the Abbassides, had no sooner learned that there existed in Egypt a scion of the illustrious family to which they still retained their attachment, than they secretly sent deputies to offer him their crown. Abderamus foresaw the obstacles with which he would be compelled to struggle, but, guided by the impulses of a soul whose native greatness had been strengthened and purified by adversity, he did not hesitate to accept the proposal of the Moors.

The Ommiade prince arrived in the Peninsula A.D. 755, Heg. 138. He speedily gained the hearts of his new subjects, assembled an army, took possession of Seville, and, soon after, marched towards Cordova, the capital of Mussulman Spain. Joseph, in the name of the Abbassides, vainly attempted to oppose his progress. The governor was vanquished and Cordova taken, together with several other cities.

Abderamus was now not only the acknowledged king of Spain, but was proclaimed *Caliph of the West* A.D. 759, Heg. 142.

During the supremacy of the Ommiades in the empire of the East, Spain had continued to be ruled by governors sent thither from Asia by those sovereigns; but it was now permanently separated from the great Arabian empire, and elevated into a powerful and independent state, acknowledging no farther allegiance to the Asiatic caliphs either in civil or religious matters. Thus was the control hitherto exercised over the affairs of Spain by the Oriental caliphs for ever wrested from them by the last surviving individual of that royal race whom Abdalla had endeavoured to exterminate.

Abderamus the First established the seat of his new greatness at Cordova. He was not long allowed peacefully to enjoy it, however. Revolts instigated by the Abbassides, incursions into Catalonia by the French, and wars with the kings of Leon,* incessantly demanded his attention; but his courage and activity gained the ascendency even over such numerous enemies. He maintained his throne with honour, and merited his beautiful surname of *The Just*.

Abderamus cultivated and cherished the fine arts, even in the midst of the difficulties and dangers by which he was surrounded. It was he who first established schools at Cordova for the study of astronomy, mathematics, medicine, and grammar. He was also a poet, and was considered the most eloquent man of his age.

This first Caliph of the West adorned and fortified his capital, erected a superb palace, which he surrounded by beautiful gardens, and commenced the construction of a grand mosque, the

* See note D, page 212.

remains of which continue even at this day to excite the admiration of the traveller. This monument of magnificence was completed during the reign of Hacchem, the son and successor of Abderamus. It is thought that the Spaniards have not preserved more than one half of the original structure, yet it is now six hundred feet long and two hundred wide, and is supported by more than three hundred columns of alabaster, jasper, and marble. Formerly there were twenty-four doors of entrance, composed of bronze covered with sculptures of gold; and nearly five thousand lamps nightly served to illuminate this magnificent edifice.

In this mosque the caliphs of Cordova each Friday conducted the worship of the people, that being the day consecrated to religion by the precepts of Mohammed. Thither all the Mussulmans of Spain made pilgrimages, as those of the East resorted to the temple at Mecca. There they celebrated, with great solemnity, the fête of the great and the lesser Beiram, which corresponds with the Passover of the Jews; that of the Newyear, and that of Miloud, or the anniversary of the birth of Mohammed. Each of these festivals lasted for eight days. During that time all labour ceased, the people sent presents to each other, exchanged visits, and offered sacrifices. Disunited families, forgetting their differences, pledged themselves to future concord, and consummated their renewed amity by delivering themselves up to the enjoyment of every pleasure permitted by the laws of the Koran.

At night the city was illuminated, the streets were festooned with flowers, and the promenades and public places resounded with the melody of various musical instruments.

The more worthily to celebrate the occasion, alms were lavishly distributed by the wealthy, and the benedictions of the poor mingled with the songs of rejoicing that everywhere ascended around them.

Abderamus, having imbibed with his Oriental education a fondness for these splendid fêtes, first introduced a taste for them into Spain. Uniting, in his character of caliph, the civil and the sacerdotal authority in his own person, he regulated the religious ceremonies on such occasions, and caused them to be celebrated with all the pomp and magnificence displayed under similar circumstances by the sovereigns of Damascus.

Though the caliph of Cordova was the enemy

of the Christians, and numbered many of them among his subjects, he refrained from persecuting them, but deprived the bishoprics of their religious heads and the churches of their priests, and encouraged marriages between the Moors and Spaniards. By these means the sagacious Moslem inflicted more injury upon the true religion than could have been effected by the most rigorous severity.

Under the reign of Abderamus, the successors of Pelagius, still retaining possession of Asturia, though weakened by the internal dissensions that already began to prevail among them, were forced to submit to the payment of the humiliating tribute of a hundred young females, Abderamus refusing to grant them peace except at this price.

Master of entire Spain, from Catalonia to the two seas, the first caliph died A.D. 788, Heg. 172, after a glorious reign of thirty years, leaving the crown to his son Hacchem, the third of his eleven sons.

After the death of Abderamus the empire was disturbed by revolts, and by wars between the new caliph and his brothers, his uncles, or other princes of the royal blood. These civil wars were inevitable under a despotic government, where not even the order of succession to the throne was regulated by law. To be an aspirant to the supreme authority of the state, it was sufficient to belong to the royal race; and as each of the caliphs, almost without exception, left numerous sons, all these princes became the head of a faction, every one of them established himself in some city, and, declaring himself its sovereign, took up arms in opposition to the authority of the caliph. From this arose the innumerable petty states that were created, annihilated, and raised again with each change of sovereigns. Thus also originated the many instances of conquered, deposed, or murdered kings, that make the history of the Moors of Spain so difficult of methodical arrangement and so monotonous in the perusal.

Hacchem, and, after him, his son Abdelazis-el-Hacchem retained possession of the caliphate notwithstanding these unceasing dissensions. The former finished the beautiful mosque commenced by his father, and carried his arms into France, in which kingdom his generals penetrated as far as Narbonne. The latter, Abdelazis-el-Hacchem less fortunate than his predecessor, did not succeed in opposing the Spaniards and his refractory subjects with unvarying success. His existence terminated in the midst of national difficulties, and his son Abderamus became his successor.

Abderamus II. was a great monarch, notwithstanding the fact that, during his reign, the power of the Christians began to balance that of the Moors.

The Christians had taken advantage of the continual divisions which prevailed among their former conquerors. Alphonso the Chaste, king of Asturia, a valiant and politic monarch, had extended his dominions and refused to pay the tribute of the hundred young maidens. Ramir, the successor of Alphonso, maintained this independence, and several times defeated the Mussulmans. Navarre became a kingdom, and Aragon had its independent sovereigns, and was so fortunate as to possess a government that properly respected the rights of the people.* The governors of Catalonia, until then subjected to the kings of France, took advantage of the feebleness of Louis le Debonnaire to render themselves independent. In fine, all the north of Spain declared itself in opposition to the Moors,

* See note E, page 212.

and the south became a prey to the irruptions of the Normans.

Abderamus defended himself against all these adversaries, and obtained, by his warlike talents, the surname of *Elmonzaffer*, which signifies *the Victorious*. And, though constantly occupied by the cares of government and of successive wars, this monarch afforded encouragement to the fine arts, embellished his capital by a new mosque, and caused to be erected a superb aqueduct, from which water was carried in leaden pipes throughout the city in the utmost abundance.

Abderamus possessed a soul capable of enjoying the most refined and elevated pleasures. He attracted to his court poets and philosophers, with whose society he frequently delighted himself; thus cultivating in his own person the talents he encouraged in others. He invited from the East the famous musician Ali-Zeriab, who established himself in Spain through the beneficence of the caliph, and originated the celebrated school* whose pupils afterward afforded such delight to the Oriental world.

The natural ferocity of the Moslems yielded to the influence of the chivalrous example of

* See note F, page 212.

the caliph, and Cordova became, under the dominion of Abderamus, the home of taste and pleasure, as well as the chosen abode of science and the arts.

A single anecdote will serve to illustrate the tenderness and generosity that so strongly characterized this illustrious descendant of the Ommiades.

One day a favourite female slave left her master's presence in high displeasure, and, retiring to her apartment, vowed that, sooner than open the door for the admittance of Abderamus, she would suffer it to be walled up. The chief eunuch, alarmed at this discourse, which he regarded as almost blasphemous, hastened to prostrate himself before the Prince of Believers, and to communicate to him the horrible purpose of the rebellious slave. Abderamus smiled at the resolution of the offended beauty, and commanded the eunuch to cause a wall composed of pieces of coin to be erected before the door of her retreat, and avowed his intention not to pass this barrier until the fair slave should have voluntarily demolished it, by possessing herself of the materials of which it was formed. The historian* adds, that the same evening the caliph entered the apartments of the appeased favourite without opposition.

This prince left forty-five sons and nearly as many daughters. Mohammed, the eldest of his sons, succeeded him, A.D. 852, Heg. 238. The reigns of Mohammed and his successors, Almanzor and Abdalla, offer to the historian nothing for a period of fifty years but details of an uninterrupted continuation of troubles, civil wars, and revolts, by which the governors of the principal cities sought to render themselves independent.

Alphonso the Great, king of Asturia, profited by these dissensions the more effectually to confirm his own power. The Normans, from another side, ravaged Andalusia anew. Toledo, frequently punished, but ever rebellious, often possessed local sovereigns. Saragossa imitated the example of Toledo. The authority of the caliphs was weakened, and their empire, convulsed in every part, seemed on the point of dissolution, when Abderamus III., the nephew of Abdalla, ascended the throne of Cordova, and restored for some time its pristine splendour and power, A.D 912, Heg. 300.

* Cardonne, in his History of Spain.

This monarch, whose name, so dear to the Moslems, seemed to be an auspicious omen, took the title of *Emir-al-Mumenim*, which signifies *Prince of true Believers*.

Victory attended the commencement of his reign; the rebels, whom his predecessors had been unable to reduce to submission, were defeated; factions were dissipated, and peace and order re-established.

Being attacked by the Christians soon after he had assumed the crown, Abderamus applied for assistance to the Moors of Africa. He maintained long wars against the kings of Leon and the counts of Castile, who wrested Madrid, then a place of comparative insignificance, from him, A.D. 931, Heg. 319. Often attacked and sometimes overcome, but always great and redoubtable notwithstanding occasional reverses, Abderamus knew how to repair his losses, and avail himself to the utmost of his good fortune. A profound statesman, and a brave and skilful commander, he fomented divisions among the Spanish princes, carried his arms frequently into the very centre of their states, and, having established a navy, seized, in addition, upon Ceuta and Seldjemessa on the African coast.

Notwithstanding the incessant wars which occupied him during the whole of his reign, the enormous expense to which he was subjected by the maintenance of his armies and his naval force, and the purchase of military assistance from Africa, Emir-al-Mumenim supported a luxury and splendour at his court, the details of which would seem to be the mere creations of the imagination, were they not attested by every historian of the time.

The contemporary Greek emperor, Constantine XI., wishing to oppose an enemy capable of resisting their power, to the Abbassides of Bagdad, sent ambassadors to Cordova to form an alliance with Abderamus.

The Caliph of the West, flattered that Christians should come from so distant a part of the world to request his support, signalized the occasion by the display of a gorgeous pomp which rivalled that of the most splendid Asiatic courts. He sent a suit of attendants to receive the ambassadors at Jean. Numerous corps of cavalry, magnificently mounted and attired, awaited their approach to Cordova, and a still more brilliant display of infantry lined the avenues to the palace. The courts were covered with the most superb Persian and Egyptian carpets, and the walls hung with cloth of gold. The caliph, blazing with brilliants, and seated on a dazzling throne, surrounded by his family, his viziers, and a numerous train of courtiers, received the Greek envoys in a hall in which all his treasures were displayed. The *Hadjeb*, a dignitary whose office among the Moors corresponded to that of the ancient French *mayors of the palace*, introduced the ambassadors. They prostrated themselves before Abderamus in amazement at the splendour of this array, and presented to the Moorish sovereign the letter of Constantine, written on blue parchment and enclosed in a box of gold. The caliph signed the treaty, loaded the imperial messengers with presents, and ordered that a numerous suite should accompany them even to the walls of Constantinople.

Abderamus III., though unceasingly occupied either by war or politics, was all his life enamoured of one of his wives named Zahra.* He built a city for her two miles distant from Cordova, which he named Zahra.

This place is now destroyed. It was situated

* This word signifies, in the Arabic, *Flower*, or *Ornament of the World*.

F

at the base of a high mountain, from which flowed numerous perpetual streams, whose waters ran in all directions through the streets of the city, diffusing health and coolness in their course, and forming ever-flowing fountains in the centre of the public places. The houses, each built after the same model, were surmounted by terraces and surrounded by gardens adorned with groves of orange, laurel, and lime, and in which the myrtle, the rose, and the jasmine mingled in pleasing confusion with all the varied productions of that sunny and delicious clime. The statue of the beautiful Zahra* was conspicuously placed over the principal gate of this City of Love.

But the attractions of the city were totally eclipsed by those of the fairy-like palace of the favourite. Abderamus, as the ally of their Imperial master, demanded the assistance of the most accomplished of the Greek architects; and the sovereign of Constantinople, which was at that time the chosen home of the fine arts, eagerly complied with his desires, and sent the caliph, in addition, forty columns of granite of the rarest and most beautiful workmanship. Independent

* See Note G, page 213.

of these magnificent columns, there were employed in the construction of this palace more than twelve hundred others, formed of Spanish and Italian marble. The walls of the apartment named the *Saloon of the Caliphate,* were covered with ornaments of gold; and from the mouths of several animals, composed of the same metal, gushed jets of water that fell into an alabaster fountain, above which was suspended the famous pearl that the Emperor Leo had presented to the caliph as a treasure of inestimable value. In the pavilion where the mistress of this enchanting abode usually passed the evening with the royal Moor, the ceiling was composed of gold and burnished steel, incrusted with precious stones. And in the resplendent light reflected from these brilliant ornaments by a hundred crystal lustres, flashed the waters of a fountain, formed like a sheaf of grain, from polished silver, whose delicate spray was received again by the alabaster basin from whose centre it sprung.

The reader might hesitate to believe these recitals; might suppose himself perusing Oriental tales, or that the author was indebted for his history to the *Thousand and One Nights,* were not the facts here detailed attested by the Arabian writers, and corroborated by foreign authors of unquestionable veracity. It is true that the architectural magnificence, the splendid pageantry, the pomp of power that characterized the reign of this illustrious Saracenic king, resembled nothing with which we are now familiar; but the incredulous questioners of their former existence might be asked whether, had the pyramids of Egypt been destroyed by an earthquake, they would now credit historians who should give us the exact dimensions of those stupendous structures?

The writers from whom are derived the details that have been given concerning the court of the Spanish Mussulmans, mention also the sums expended in the erection of the palace and city of Zahra. The cost amounted annually to three hundred thousand dinars of gold,* and twenty-five years hardly sufficed for the completion of this princely monument of chivalrous devotion.

* The *dinar* is estimated by M. Florian to be equal to at least *ten livres*. According to that computation, the aggregate cost of the palace and city of Zahra would amount to considerably more than $14,000,000. *Trans.*

To these enormous expenditures should be added the maintenance of a seraglio, in which the women, the slaves, and the black and white eunuchs amounted to the number of six thousand persons. The officers of the court, and the horses destined for their use, were in equally lavish proportion. The royal guard alone was composed of twelve thousand cavaliers.

When it is remembered, that, from being continually at war with the Spanish princes, Abderamus was obliged to keep numerous armies incessantly on foot, to support a naval force, frequently to hire stipendiaries from Africa, and to fortify and preserve in a state of defence the ever-endangered fortresses on his frontiers, it is hardly possible to comprehend how his revenues sufficed for the supply of such immense and varied demands. But his resources were equally immense and varied; and the sovereign of Cordova was perhaps the richest and most powerful monarch then in Europe.*

He held possession of Portugal, Andalusia, the kingdom of Grenada, Mercia, Valencia, and the greater part of New-Castile, the most beautiful and fertile countries of Spain.

* See note H, page 214.

These provinces were at that time extremely populous, and the Moors had attained the highest perfection in agriculture. Historians assure us, that there existed on the shores of the Guadalquiver twelve thousand villages; and that a traveller could not proceed through the country without encountering some hamlet every quarter of an hour. There existed in the dominions of the caliph eighty great cities, three hundred of the second order, and an infinite number of smaller towns. Cordova, the capital of the kingdom, enclosed within its walls two hundred thousand houses and nine hundred public baths.

All this prosperity was reversed by the expulsion of the Moors from the Peninsula. The reason is apparent: the Moorish conquerors of Spain did not persecute their vanquished foes; the Spaniards, when they had subdued the Moors, oppressed and banished them.

The revenues of the caliphs of Cordova are represented to have amounted annually to twelve millions and forty-five thousand *dinars* of gold.*
Independent of this income in money, many imposts were paid in the products of the soil; and among an industrious agricultural popula-

* About $22,500,000.

tion, possessed of the most fertile country in the world, this rural wealth was incalculable. The gold and silver mines, known in Spain from the earliest times, were another source of wealth. Commerce, too, enriched alike the sovereign and the people. The commerce of the Moors was carried on in many articles: silks, oils, sugar, cochineal, iron, wool (which was at that time extremely valuable), ambergris, yellow amber, loadstone, antimony, isinglass, rock-crystal, sulphur, saffron, ginger, the product of the coral-beds on the coast of Andalusia, of the pearl fisheries on that of Catalonia, and rubies, of which they had discovered two localities, one at Malaga and another at Beja. These valuable articles were, either before or after being wrought, transported to Egypt or other parts of Africa, and to the East. The emperors of Constantinople, always allied from necessity to the caliphs of Cordova, favoured these commercial enterprises, and, by their countenance, assisted in enlarging, to a vast extent, the field of their operations; while the neighbourhood of Africa, Italy, and France contributed also to their prosperity.

The arts, which are the children of commerce, and support the existence of their parent, added a new splendour to the brilliant reign of Abderamus. The superb palaces he erected, the delicious gardens he created, and the magnificent fêtes he instituted, drew to his court from all parts architects and artists of every description. Cordova was the home of industry and the asylum of the sciences. Celebrated schools of geometry, astronomy, chymistry, and medicine were established there—schools which, a century afterward, produced such men as Averroes and Abenzoar. So distinguished were the learned Moorish poets, philosophers, and physicians, that Alphonso the Great, king of Asturia, wishing to confide the care of his son Ordogno to teachers capable of conducting the education of a prince, appointed him two Arabian preceptors, notwithstanding the difference of religious faith, and the hatred entertained by the Christians towards the Mussulmans. And one of the successors of Alphonso, Sancho the Great, king of Leon, being attacked by a disease which it was supposed would prove fatal in its effects, went unhesitatingly to Cordova, claimed the hospitality of his national enemy, and placed himself under the care of the Mohammedan physicians, who eventually succeeded in curing the malady of the Christian king.

This singular fact does as much honour to the skill of the learned Saracens as to the magnanimity of the caliph and the trusting confidence of Sancho.

Such was the condition of the caliphate of Cordova under the dominion of Abderamus III. He occupied the throne fifty years, and we have seen with what degree of honour to himself and benefit to his people. Perhaps nothing will better illustrate the superiority of this prince to monarchs generally than the following fragment, which was found, traced by his own hand, among his papers after his death.

"Fifty years have passed away since I became caliph. Riches, honours, pleasures, I have enjoyed them all: I am satiated with them all. Rival kings respect me, fear, and envy me. All that the heart of man can desire, Heaven has lavishly bestowed on me. In this long period of seeming felicity I have estimated the number of days during which I have enjoyed *perfect happiness*: they amount to *fourteen!* Mortals, learn to appreciate greatness, the world, and human life!"

The successor of this monarch was his eldest

son, Aboul-Abbas El Hakkam, who assumed, like his father, the title of *Emir-al-Mumenim*.

The coronation of El Hakkam was celebrated with great pomp in the city of Zahra. The new caliph there received the oath of fidelity from the chiefs of the scythe guard, a numerous and redoubtable corps, composed of strangers, which Abderamus III. had formed. The brothers and relations of El Hakkam, the viziers and their chief, the *Hadjeb*, the white and black eunuchs, the archers and cuirassiers of the guard, all swore obedience to the monarch. These ceremonies were followed by the funeral honours of Abderamus, whose body was carried to Cordova, and there deposited in the tomb of his ancestors.

Aboul-Abbas El Hakkam, equally wise with his father, but less warlike than he, enjoyed greater tranquillity during his reign. His was the dominion of justice and peace. The success and vigilance of Abderamus had extinguished, for a time, the spirit of revolt, and prepared the way for the continued possession of these great national blessings.

Divided among themselves, the Christian kings entertained no designs of disturbing their infidel neighbours.

The truce that existed between the Mussulmans and Castile and Leon was broken but once during the life of El Hacchem. The caliph then commanded his army in person, and completed a glorious campaign, taking several cities from the Spaniards, and convincing them, by his achievements, of the policy of future adherence to the terms of their treaty with their Saracen opponents.

During the remainder of his reign the Moorish sovereign applied himself wholly to promoting the happiness of his subjects, to the cultivation of science, to the collection of an extensive library, and, above all, to enforcing a strict observance of the laws.

The laws of the Moors were few and simple. It does not appear that there existed among them any civil laws apart from those incorporated with their religious code. Jurisprudence was reduced to the application of the principles contained in the Koran. The caliph, as the supreme head of their religion, possessed the power of interpreting these principles; but even he would not have ventured to violate them. At least as often as once a week, he publicly gave audience to his subjects, listened to their complaints, examined the guilty, and, without quitting the tribunal, caused punishment to be immediately inflicted. The governors placed by the sovereign over the different cities and provinces, commanded the military force belonging to each, collected the public revenues, superintended the administration of the police, and adjudged the offences committed within their respective governments. Public officers well versed in the laws discharged the functions of notaries, and gave a juridical form to records relating to the possession of property. When any lawsuits arose, magistrates called *cadis*, whose authority was respected both by the king and the people, could alone decide them. These suits were speedily determined; lawyers and attorneys were unknown, and there was no expense nor chicanery connected with them. Each party pleaded his cause in person, and the decrees of the cadi were immediately executed.

Criminal jurisprudence was scarcely more complicated. The Moors almost invariably resorted to the *punishment of retaliation* prescribed by the founder of their religion. In truth, the wealthy were permitted to exonerate themselves from the charge of bloodshed by the aid of money; but it was necessary that the relations of the deceased should consent to this: the caliph himself would not have ventured to withhold the head of one of his own sons who had been guilty of homicide, if its delivery had been inexorably insisted upon.

This simple code would not have sufficed had not the unlimited authority exercised by fathers over their children, and husbands over their wives, supplied the deficiencies of the laws. With regard to this implicit obedience on the part of a family to the will of its chief, the Moors preserved the ancient patriarchal customs of their ancestors. Every father possessed, under his own roof, rights nearly equal to those of the caliph. He decided, without appeal, the quarrels of his wives and those of his sons: he punished with severity the slightest faults, and even possessed the power of punishing certain crimes with death. Age alone conferred this supremacy. An old man was always an object of reverence. His presence arrested disorders: the most haughty young man cast down his eyes at meeting him, and listened patiently to his reproofs. In short, the possessor of a white beard was everywhere invested with the authority of a magistrate.

This authority, which was more powerful among the Moors than that of their laws, long subsisted unimpaired at Cordova. That the wise Hacchem did nothing to enfeeble it, may be judged from the following illustration.

A poor woman of Zahra possessed a small field contiguous to the gardens of the caliph. El Hacchem, wishing to erect a pavilion there, directed that the owner should be requested to dispose of it to him. But the woman refused every remuneration that was offered her, and declared that she would never sell the heritage of her ancestry. The king was, doubtless, not informed of the obstinacy of this woman; but the superintendent of the palace gardens, a minister worthy of a despotic sovereign, forcibly seized upon the field, and the pavilion was built. The poor woman hastened in despair to Cordova, to relate the story of her misfortune to the Cadi Bechir, and to consult him respecting the course she should pursue. The cadi thought that the Prince of true Believers had no more right than any other man to possess himself by violence of the property of another; and he endeavoured to discover some means of recalling to his recollection a truth which the best of rulers will sometimes forget.

One day, as the Moorish sovereign was surrounded by his court in the beautiful pavilion built on the ground belonging to the poor woman, the Cadi Bechir presented himself before him, seated on an ass, and carrying in his hand a large sack. The astonished caliph demanded his errand. "Prince of the Faithful!" replied Bechir, "I come to ask permission of thee to fill this sack with the earth upon which thou standest." The caliph cheerfully consented to this desire, and the cadi filled his sack with the earth. He then left it standing, and, approaching his sovereign, entreated him to crown his goodness by aiding him in loading his ass with its burden. El Hacchem, amused by the request, yielded to it, and attempted to raise the sack. Scarcely able to move it, he let it fall again, and, laughing, complained of its enormous weight. "Prince of Believers!" said Bechir then, with impressive gravity, "this sack, which thou findest so heavy, contains, nevertheless, but a small portion of the field thou hast usurped from one of thy subjects; how wilt thou sustain the weight of this entire field when thou shalt appear in the presence of the Great Judge charged with this iniquity?" The caliph, struck with this address, embraced the cadi, thanked him, acknowledged his fault, and immediately restored to the poor woman the field of which she had been despoiled, together with the pavilion and everything it contained.

The praise due to a despotic sovereign capable of such an action, is inferior only to that which should be accorded to the cadi who induced him to perform it.

After reigning twelve years, El Hakkam died, A.D. 976, Heg. 366. His son Hacchem succeeded him.

This prince was an infant when he ascended the throne, and his intellectual immaturity continued through life. During and after his minority, a celebrated Moor named Mohammed Almanzor, being invested with the important office of *Hadjeb*, governed the state with wisdom and success.

Almanzor united to the talents of a statesman the genius of a great commander. He was the most formidable and fatal enemy with whom the Christians had yet been obliged to contend. He ruled the Moorish empire twenty-six years under the name of the indolent Hacchem. More than fifty different times he carried the terrors of war into Castile or Asturia: he took and sacked the cities of Barcelona and Leon, and advanced even to Compostella, destroying its famous church and carrying the spoils to Cordova.

The genius and influence of Mohammed temporarily restored the Moors to their ancient strength and energy, and forced the whole Peninsula to respect the rights of his feeble master, who, like another Sardanapalus, dreamed away his life in the enjoyment of effeminate and debasing pleasures.*

But this was the last ray of unclouded splendour that shone upon the empire of the Ommiades in Spain. The kings of Leon and Navarre, and the Count of Castile, united their forces for the purpose of opposing the redoubtable Almanzor.

The opposing armies met near Medina-Celi. The conflict was long and sanguinary, and the victory doubtful. The Moors, after the termination of the combat, took to flight, terrified by the fearful loss they had sustained; and Alman-

* See Note I, page 214.

G

zor, whom fifty years of uninterrupted military success had persuaded that he was invincible, died of grief at this first mortifying reverse.

With this great man expired the good fortune of the Saracens of Spain. From the period of his death, the Spaniards continued to increase their own prosperity by the gradual ruin of the Moors.

The sons of the hadjeb Almanzor successively replaced their illustrious father; but, in inheriting his power, they did not inherit his talents. Factions were again created. One of the relations of the caliph took up arms against him, and possessed himself of the person of the monarch, A.D. 1005, Heg. 596; and, though the rebellious prince dared not sacrifice the life of Hacchem, he imprisoned him, and spread a report of his death.

This news reaching Africa, an Ommiade prince hastened thence to Spain with an army, under pretext of avenging the death of Hacchem. The Count of Castile formed an alliance with this stranger, and civil war was kindled in Cordova. It soon spread throughout Spain, and the Christian princes availed themselves of its disastrous effects to repossess themselves of the cities of which they had been deprived during the supremacy of Almanzor.

The imbecile Hacchem, negotiating and trifling alike with all parties, was finally replaced on the throne, but was soon after forced again to renounce it to save his life.

After this event a multitude of conspirators* were in turn proclaimed caliph, and in turn deposed, poisoned, or otherwise murdered. Almundir, the last lingering branch of the race of the Ommiades, was bold enough to claim the restoration of the rights of his family, even amid the tumult of conflicting parties. His friends represented to him the dangers he was about to encounter. " Should I reign but one day," replied he, " and expire on the next, I would not murmur at my fate!" But the desire of the prince, even to this extent, was not gratified; he was assassinated without obtaining possession of the caliphate.

Usurpers of momentary authority followed. Jalmar-ben-Mohammed was the last in order. His death terminated the empire of the Caliphs

* Mahadi, Suleiman, Ali, Abderamus IV., Casim, Jahiah, Hacchem III., Mohammed, Abderamus V., Jahiah II., Hacchem IV., and Jalmar-ben-Mohammed.

of the West, which had been possessed by the dynasty of the Ommiades for the period of three centuries, A.D. 1027, Heg. 416.

With the extinction of this line of princes vanished the power and the glory of Cordova.

The governors of the different cities, who had hitherto been the vassals of the court of Cordova, profiting by the anarchy that prevailed, erected themselves into independent sovereigns.— That city was therefore no longer the capital of a kingdom, though it still retained the religious supremacy which it derived from its mosque.

Enfeebled by divisions and subjected to such diversity of rule, the Mussulmans were no longer able successfully to resist the encroachments of the Spaniards. The Third Epoch of their history, therefore, will present nothing but a narrative of their rapid decline.

THIRD EPOCH.

CONTAINING AN ACCOUNT OF THE PRINCIPAL KINGDOMS THAT SPRANG FROM THE RUINS OF THE CALIPHATE.

Extending from the Commencement of the Eleventh to the Middle of the Thirteenth Century.

AT the commencement of the eleventh century, when the throne of Cordova was daily stained by the blood of some new usurper, the governors of the different cities, as has been already remarked, had assumed the title of kings. Toledo, Saragossa, Seville, Valencia, Lisbon, Huesca, and several other places of inferior importance, each possessed independent sovereigns.

The history of these numerous kingdoms would be nearly as fatiguing to the reader as to the writer. It presents, for the space of two hundred years, nothing but accounts of repeated massacres, of fortresses taken and retaken, of pillages and seditions, of occasional instances of heroic conduct, but far more numerous crimes. Passing rapidly over two centuries of misfortunes, let it suffice to contemplate the termination of these petty Moorish sovereignties.

Christian Spain, in the mean time, presented nearly the same picture as that exhibited by the portion of the Peninsula still in possession of the Mohammedans. The kings of Leon, Navarre, Castile, and Aragon were almost always relatives, and sometimes brothers; but they were not, for that reason, the less sanguinary in their designs towards each other. Difference of religion did not prevent them from uniting with the Moors, the more effectually to oppress other Christians, or other Moors with whom they chanced to be at enmity. Thus, in a battle which occurred A.D. 1010 between two Mussulman leaders, there were found among the slain a count of Urgel and three bishops of Catalonia.* And the King of Leon, Alphonso V., gave his sister Theresa in marriage to Abdalla, the Moorish king of Toledo, to convert him into an ally against Castile.

Among the Christians, as among the Moors, crimes were multiplied; civil wars of both a local and general nature at the same time distracted Spain, and the unhappy people expiated with

* See note A, page 216

their property and their lives the iniquities of their rulers.

While thus regarding a long succession of melancholy events, it is agreeable to find a king of Toledo called Almamon, and Benabad, the Mussulman king of Seville, affording an asylum at their courts, the one to Alphonso, the young king of Leon, and the other to the unfortunate Garcias, king of Galicia, both of whom had been driven from their kingdoms by their brother Sancho, of Castile, A.D. 1071 Heg. 465. Sancho pursued his brothers as though they had been his most implacable enemies; and the Moorish monarchs, the natural enemies of all the Christians, received these two fugitive princes as brothers. Almamon, especially, lavished the most affectionate attention upon the unfortunate Alphonso: he endeavoured to entertain him at Toledo with such varied pleasures as should banish regret for the loss of a throne : he gave him an income, and, in short, treated the prince as though he had been a near and beloved relative. When the death of the cruel Sancho (A.D. 1072, Heg. 466) had rendered Alphonso king of Leon and Castile, the generous Almamon, who now had the person of the king of his enemies in his power, accompanied the prince to the frontiers of his kingdom, loaded him with presents and caresses, and, at parting, offered the free use of his troops and treasures to his late guest.

While Almamon lived, Alphonso IV. never forgot his obligations to his benefactor. He maintained peace with him, aided him in his campaigns against the King of Seville, and even entered into a treaty with Hacchem, the son and successor of his ally. But, after a brief reign, Hacchem left the throne of Toledo to his youthful brother Jahiah. That prince oppressed the Christians, who were very numerous in his city; and they secretly implored Alphonso to make war upon Jahiah. The memory of Almamon long caused the Spanish monarch to hesitate in relation to this subject. Gratitude impelled him not to listen to the suggestions of ambition and the prayers of his countrymen; but the arguments of gratitude proved the least strong, and Alphonso encamped before Toledo.

After a long and celebrated siege, to which several French and other foreign warriors eagerly hastened, Toledo finally capitulated, A.D 1085, Heg. 478.

The conqueror allowed the sons of Almamon

to go and reign at Valencia, and engaged by an oath to preserve the mosques from destruction. He could not, however, prevent the Christians from speedily violating this promise.

Such was the end of the Moorish kingdom of Toledo. This ancient capital of the Goths had belonged to the Arabs three hundred and eighty two years.

Several other less important cities now submitted to the Christian yoke. The kings of Aragon and Navarre, and the Count of Barcelona, incessantly harassed and besieged the petty Mussulman princes who still remained in the north of Spain. The attacks of the kings of Castile and Leon afforded sufficient occupation for those of the south, effectually to prevent their rendering any assistance to their brethren. Above all, the Cid, the famous Cid, flew from one part of Spain to another, at the head of the invincible band with whom his fame had surrounded him, everywhere achieving victories for the Christians, and even lending the aid of his arms to the Moors when they were internally divided, but always securing success to the party he favoured.

This hero, one of the most truly admirable of those whom history has celebrated, since in his character were united the most exalted virtue and the highest qualities of the soldier; this simple Castilian cavalier, upon whom his reputation alone bestowed the control of armies, became master of several cities, assisted the King of Aragon to seize upon Huesca, and conquered the kingdom of Valencia without any other assistance than that of his men-at-arms. Equal in power with his sovereign, of whose treatment he frequently had reason to complain, and envied and persecuted by the jealous courtiers, the Cid never forgot for a moment that he was the subject of the King of Castile. Banished from court, and even exiled from his estates, he hastened, with his brave companions, to attack and conquer the Moors, and to send those of them whom he vanquished to render homage to the king who had deprived him of his rights.

Being soon recalled to the presence of Alphonso, in consequence of the king's needing his military aid, the Cid left the scenes of his martial triumphs, and, without demanding reparation for the injuries he had sustained, returned to defend his persecutors; ever ready, while in disgrace, to forget everything in the performance of his duty to his king, and equally ready, when enjoying the favour of the sovereign, to displease him, if it should be necessary to do so, by advocating the cause of truth and justice.*

While the prowess of the Cid maintained the contest, the Christians had the advantage; but a few years after his death, which occurred in the year 1099 and the 492d of the Hegira, the Moors of Andalusia changed masters, and became, for a time, more formidable than ever to their Spanish foes.

After the fall of Toledo, Seville had increased in power. The sovereigns of that city were also masters of ancient Cordova, and possessed, in addition, Estremadura and a part of Portugal. Benabad, king of Seville, one of the most estimable princes of his age, was now the only one of its enemies capable of disturbing the safety of Castile. Alphonso IV., desirous of allying himself with this powerful Moor, demanded his daughter in marriage. His proposal was acceded to, and the Castilian monarch received several towns as the dowry of the Moorish princess; but this extraordinary union, which seemed to ensure peace between the two nations, nevertheless soon became either the cause or the pretext of renewed contests.

* See note B, page 216.

Africa, after having been separated from the vast empire of the Caliphs of the East by the Fatimite caliphs, and being, during three centuries of civil war, the prey of a succession of conquerors more ferocious and sanguinary than the lions of their deserts,* was now subjected to the family of the *Almoravides*, a powerful tribe of Egyptian origin. Joseph-ben-Tessefin, the second prince of this dynasty, founded the kingdom and city of Morocco.

Endowed with some warlike talents, proud of his power, and burning to augment it, Joseph regarded with a covetous eye the beautiful European provinces which had formerly been conquered by the Mussulmans of Africa.

Some historians assert that the King of Castile, Alphonso IV., and his father-in-law Benabad, king of Seville, having formed the project of dividing Spain between them, committed the capital error of summoning the Moors of Africa to their assistance in this grand design. But others, founding their assertions upon more plausible reasoning, say that the petty Mussulman kings, who were the neighbours or tributaries of Benabad, justly alarmed at his alliance with a

* See note C, page 218.

Christian king, solicited the support of the Almoravide.

But, be that as it may, the ambitious Joseph eagerly availed himself of the fortunate pretext presented by the invitation he had received, and crossed the Mediterranean at the head of an army. He hastened to attack Alphonso, and succeeded in overcoming him in a battle that took place between them, A.D. 1097, Heg. 490. Then turning his arms against Benabad, Joseph took Cordova, besieged Seville, and was preparing for the assault of that city, when the virtuous Benabad, sacrificing his crown and even his liberty to save his subjects from the horrors that threatened them, delivered himself up, together with his family of a hundred children, to the disposal of the Almoravide.

The barbarous African, dreading the influence of a monarch whose virtues had rendered him so justly dear to his people, sent him to end his days in an African prison, where his daughters were obliged to support their father and brothers by the labour of their hands.

The unfortunate Benabad lived six years after the commencement of his imprisonment, regretting his lost throne only for the sake of his people, and beguiling the period of his protracted leisure by the composition of several poems which are still in existence. In them he attempts to console his daughters under their heavy afflictions, recalls the remembrance of his vanished greatness, and offers himself as a warning and example to kings who shall presume to trust too confidently to the unchanging continuance of the favours of fortune.

Joseph-ben-Tessefin, after he had thus become master of Seville and Cordova, soon succeeded in subjugating the other petty Mussulman states; and the Moors, united under a single monarch as powerful as Joseph, threatened again to occupy the important position they had sustained during the supremacy of their caliphs. The Spanish princes, alarmed at this prospect, suspended their individual quarrels, and joined Alphonso in resisting the Africans.

At this particular juncture, a fanatical love of religion and glory induced many European warriors to take up arms against the infidels. Raymond of Bourgogne, and his kinsman Henry, both French princes of the blood, Raymond of Saint-Gilles, count of Toulouse, with some other cavaliers from among their vassals, crossed the

Pyrenees with their retainers, and fought under the banners of the King of Castile. Thus assisted, that sovereign put the Egyptian commander to flight, and compelled him, soon afterward, to recross the Mediterranean.

The grateful Alphonso gave his daughters as a recompense to the distinguished Frenchmen who had lent him the aid of their arms. The eldest, Urraca, espoused Raymond of Bourgogne, and their son afterward inherited the kingdom of Castile. Theresa became the wife of Henry, and brought him as a dowry all the land he had thus far conquered or should hereafter conquer in Portugal: from thence originated that kingdom. Elvira was given to Raymond, count of Toulouse, who carried her with him to the Holy Land, where he gained some possessions by his valour.

Excited by these illustrious examples, other French cavaliers resorted soon after to the standard of the King of *Aragon*, Alphonso I., who made himself master of Saragossa, and for ever destroyed that ancient kingdom of the Moors, A.D. 1118, Heg. 512.

The son of Henry of Bourgogne, Alphonso 1. king of Portugal, a prince renowned for his bravery, availed himself of the presence of a combined fleet of English, Flemings, and Germans, who had anchored in the harbour of that city on their way to the Holy Land, to lay siege to Lisbon. He carried that place by assault, in spite of its great strength, and made it the capital of his kingdom, A.D. 1147, Heg. 541.

During this period the kings of Castile and Navarre were extending their conquests in Andalusia.

The Moors were attacked on all sides, and their cities were everywhere compelled to surrender, now that they were no longer materially aided by the Almoravides. Those African princes were at this time sufficiently occupied at home in opposing some new sectaries, the principal of whom, under pretext of reinitiating the people in a knowledge of the pure doctrines of Mohammed, opened for themselves a path to the throne, and, after many struggles, ended by effectually driving the family of the Almoravides from its possession. The new conquerors, becoming by these means masters of Morocco and Fez, destroyed, according to the African custom, every individual of the supplanted race, and founded a new dynasty, which is known under the name of the *Almohades*, A.D. 1149, Heg. 543.

In the midst of these divisions, these wars and combats, the fine arts still continued to be cultivated at Cordova. And though they were no longer in the flourishing condition in which they were maintained during the reigns of the several caliphs who bore the cherished name of Abderamus, yet the schools of philosophy, poetry, and medicine had continued to exist. These schools produced, in the twelfth century, several distinguished men, among the most celebrated of whom were the learned Abenzoar and the famous Averroes. The former, equally profound in medicine, pharmacy, and surgery, lived, it is said, to the age of one hundred and thirty-five years. Some estimable works which he produced are still extant. Averroes was also a physician, but he was more of a philosopher, poet, lawyer, and commentator. He acquired a reputation so profound, that passing centuries have only served more firmly to establish it. The disposition made by this remarkable man of his time during the different periods of his existence, will illustrate his mental character, In his youth he was the passionate votary of pleasure and poetry: in more mature age he burned the verses he had previously composed, studied the principles of legislation, and discharged the duties of a judicial officer: having advanced still farther in life, he abandoned these occupations for the pursuit of medicine, in which he attained very great eminence: at last philosophy alone supplied the place of every earlier taste, and wholly engrossed his attention for the remainder of his life. It was Averroes who first created among the Moors a taste for Greek literature. He translated the works of Aristotle into Arabic, and wrote commentaries upon them. He also published several other works upon philosophy and medicine, and possessed the united glory of having both enlightered and benefited mankind.*

As Africa, distracted by the long war of the Almoravides and the Almohades, was unable to offer any opposition to the progress of the Christians in Spain, these last, availing themselves of this condition of affairs, continued to extend their conquests in Andalusia. If the Spanish princes had been less disunited, and had acted in concert against the infidels, they would have been able

* See Note D, page 220.

at this period to deprive the Mussulmans of their entire dominions in the Peninsula. But these ever-contending princes had no sooner taken a Moorish city than they began to dispute among themselves about its possession.

The newly-created kingdom of Portugal, established by the military powers of Alphonso, was soon at war with that of Leon.* Aragon and Castile, after many bloody quarrels, united in a league against Navarre. Sancho VIII., the sovereign of that little state, was forced to resort to Africa for assistance, and implore the aid of the Almohades. But they, being but recently established on the throne of Morocco, were still employed in exterminating the dismembered fragments of the party of the Almoravides, and could not, in spite of their eager desire to do so, establish any claim to their assumed rights in Spain. Nevertheless, two kings of the race of the Almohades, both named Joseph, passed the Mediterranean more than once with numerous armies. The one was successfully opposed by the Portuguese, and did not survive his final defeat; the other was more fortunate, and succeeded in vanquishing the Castilians, but

* A.D. 1178.

was soon after obliged to accept a truce and return in haste to Morocco, to which new disturbances recalled him, A.D. 1195, Heg. 591.

But these useless victories, these ill-sustained efforts, did not permanently disable either the Mussulmans or the Christians. On both sides, the vanquished parties soon re-entered the field, in utter neglect of the treaties into which they might ever so recently have entered. The sovereigns of Morocco, though regarded as the kings of Andalusia, nevertheless possessed only a precarious authority in that country, which was always disputed when they were absent, and acknowledged only when necessity forced the Mussulman inhabitants to have recourse to their protection.

At last Mohammed *El Nazir*, the fourth prince of the dynasty of the Almohades, to whom the Spaniards gave the name of the *Green*, from the colour of his turban, finding himself in quiet possession of the Moorish empire of Africa, resolved to assemble all his forces, to lead them into Spain, and to renew in that country the ancient conquests of Tarik and Moussa. A holy war was proclaimed, A.D. 1211, Heg 608, and an innumerable army crowded around the ensigns of Mohammed, left the snores of Africa under the guidance of that monarch, and safely arrived in Andalusia. There their numbers were nearly doubled by the Spanish Moors, whom hatred to the very name of Christian, arising from the vivid remembrance of accumulated injuries, induced to join the bands of El Nazir.

The sanguine Mohammed promised an easy triumph to his followers, together with the certainty of rendering themselves masters of all that their ancestors had formerly possessed; and, burning to commence the contest, he immediately advanced towards Castile at the head of his formidable army, which, according to the reports of historians, amounted to more than six hundred thousand men.

The king of Castile, Alphonso the Noble, informed of the warlike preparations of the King of Morocco, implored the assistance of the Christian princes of Europe. Pope Innocent III. proclaimed a crusade and granted indulgences most lavishly. Rodrique, archbishop of Toledo, made in person a voyage to Rome, to solicit the aid of the sovereign pontiff; and, returning homeward through France, preached to the people on his route, and induced many cavaliers to proceed at the head of bands of recruits to Spain, and join the opponents of the Mussulmans.

The general rendezvous was at Toledo, at which point there were soon collected more than sixty thousand crusaders from Italy and France, who united themselves with the soldiers of Castile. The King of Aragon, Peter II., the same who afterward perished in the war of the Albigense, led his valiant army to the place of meeting, and Sancho VIII., king of Navarre, was not backward in presenting himself at the head of his brave subjects. The Portuguese had recently lost their king, but they despatched their best warriors to Toledo. In short, all Spain flew to arms. There was general union for the promotion of mutual safety; for never, since the time of King Rodrique, had the Christians been placed in such imminent danger.

It was at the foot of the Sierra Morena, at a place named *Las Navas de Toloza*, that the three Spanish princes encountered the Moors, A.D. 1212, Heg. 609.

Mohammed El Nazir had taken possession of the mountain gorges through which it had been the intention of the Christians to approach his camp. The adroit African thus designed, either to force his opponents to turn back, which would expose them to the danger of a failure of provisions, or to overwhelm them in the pass if they should attempt to enter it. Upon discovering this circumstance, a council was called by the embarrassed Christian leaders. Alphonso was desirous of attempting the passage, but the kings of Navarre and Aragon advised a retreat. In the midst of this dilemma, a shepherd presented himself before them, and offered to conduct them through a defile of the mountain, with which he was familiar. This proposal, which was the salvation of their army, was eagerly accepted, and the shepherd guided the Catholic sovereigns through difficult paths and across rocks and torrents, until, with their followers, they finally succeeded in attaining the summit of the mountain.

There, suddenly presenting themselves before the eyes of the astonished Moors, they were engaged for the space of two days in preparing themselves for the conflict, by prayer, confession, and the solemn reception of the holy sacrament. Their leaders set an example to the soldiers in this zealous devotion; and the prelates and ecclesiastics, of whom there were a great number in the camp, after having absolved these devout warriors, prepared to accompany them into the midst of the conflict.

Upon the third day, the sixteenth of July, in the year twelve hundred and twelve, the Christian army was drawn up in battle array. The troops were formed into three divisions, each commanded by a king. Alphonso was in the centre, at the head of his Castilians and the chevaliers of the newly-instituted orders of Saint James and Calatrava; Rodrique, archbishop of Toledo, the eyewitness and historian of this great battle, advanced by the side of Alphonso, preceded by a large cross, the principal ensign of the army; Sancho and his Navarrois formed the right, while Peter and his subjects occupied the left. The French crusaders, now reduced to a small number by the desertion of many of their companions, who had been unable to endure the scorching heat of the climate, marched in the van of the other troops, under the command of Arnault, archbishop of Narbonne.

Thus disposed, the Christians descended towards the valley which separated them from their enemies.

The Moors, according to their ancient custom, everywhere displayed their innumerable soldiers, without order or arrangement. An admirable cavalry, to the number of a hundred thousand men, composed their principal strength: the rest of their army was made up of a crowd of ill-armed and imperfectly trained foot-soldiers. Mohammed, stationed on a height, from which he could command a view of his whole army, was encompassed by a defence made of chains of iron, guarded by the choicest of his cavaliers on foot. Standing in the midst of this enclosure, with the Koran in one hand and an unsheathed sabre in the other, the Saracen commander was visible to all his troops, of whom the bravest squadrons occupied the four sides of the hill.

The Castilians directed their first efforts towards this elevation. At first they drove back the Moors, but, repulsed in their turn, they recoiled in disorder and began to retreat. Alphonso flew here and there, attempting to rally their broken ranks. "Archbishop," said he to the prelate who everywhere accompanied him, preceded by the grand standard of the Cross, "Archbishop, here are we destined to die!"

"Not so, sire," replied the ecclesiastic; "we are destined here to live and conquer!" At that moment the brave canon who carried the chief ensign threw himself with it into the midst of the infidels; the prelate and the king followed him, and the Castilian soldiers rushed forward to protect their sovereign and their sacred standard. The already victorious kings of Aragon and Navarre now advanced at the head of their wings to unite in the attack upon the height. The Moors were assaulted at all points: they bravely resisted their opponents; but the Christians crowded upon them—the Aragonais, the Navarrois, and the Castilians endeavouring mutually to surpass each other in courage and daring. The brave King of Navarre, making a path for himself through the midst of its defenders, reached the enclosure, and struck and broke the chains by which the Moorish commander was surrounded.* Mohammed took to flight on beholding this catastrophe; and his soldiers, no longer beholding their king, lost both hope and courage. They gave way in all directions, and fled before the Christians. Thousands of the Mussulmans fell beneath the

* See Note E, page 221.

weapons of their pursuers, while the Archbishop of Toledo, with the other ecclesiastics, surrounding the victorious sovereigns, chanted a *Te Deum* on the field of battle.

Thus was gained the famous battle of Toloza, of which some details have been given in consequence of its great importance, and in illustration of the military tactics of the Moors. With them the arts of war consisted solely in mingling with the enemy, and fighting, each one for himself, until either the strongest or the bravest of the two parties remained masters of the field.

The Spaniards possessed but little more military skill than their Moslem neighbours; but their infantry, at least, could attack and resist in mass, while the discipline of that of the Saracens amounted to scarcely anything. On the other hand, again, the cavalry of the Moors was admirably trained. The cavaliers who composed it belonged to the principal families in the kingdom, and possessed excellent horses, in the art of managing which they had been trained from childhood. Their mode of combat was to rush forward with the rapidity of light, strike with the sabre or the lance, fly away as quickly, and then wheel suddenly and return again to the encounter. Thus they often succeeded in recalling victory to their standard when she seemed just about to desert them. The Christians, covered as they were with iron, had in some respects the advantage of these knights, whose persons were protected only by a breastplate and headpiece of steel. The Moorish foot-soldiers were nearly naked, and armed only with a wretched pike. It is easy to perceive that, when involved in the *mêlée*, and, above all, during a route, vast numbers of them must have perished. This, too, renders less incredible the seemingly extravagant accounts given by historians of their losses in the field. They assert, for example, that, at the battle of Toloza, the Christians killed two hundred thousand Moors, while they lost themselves but fifteen hundred soldiers. Even when these assertions are estimated at their true value, it remains certain that the infidels sustained an immense loss; and this important defeat, which is still celebrated yearly at Toledo by a solemn fête, long deprived the kings of Morocco of all hope of subjugating the Spaniards.

The victory of Toloza was followed by more fatal consequences to the unfortunate Mohammed than to the Moors of Andalusia; for the latter retired to their cities, defended them by means of the remains of the African army, and successfully resisted the Spanish princes, who succeeded in taking but few of their strong places, and, speedily dissolving their league, separated for their respective kingdoms. But Mohammed, despised by his subjects after his defeat, and assailed by the treachery of his nearest relations, lost all authority in Spain, and beheld the principal Moors, whom he had now no power to control, again forming little states, the independence of which they were prepared to assert by force of arms.* The discomfited El Nazir consequently returned to Africa, where he soon after died of chagrin.

With Mohammed the Green vanished the good fortune of the Almohades. The princes of that house, who followed El Nazir in rapid succession, purchased their royal prerogatives at the expense of continual unhappiness and danger, and were finally driven from the throne. The empire of Morocco was then divided, and three new dynasties were established; that of Fez, of Tunis, and of Tremecen. These three powerful and rival sovereignties greatly multiplied the

* A.D. 1213, Heg. 610.

conflicts, crimes, and atrocities, the narration of which alone constitutes the history of Africa.

About this period some dissensions arose in Castile, which, together with the part assumed by the King of Aragon in the war of the Albigense in France, allowed the Moors time to breathe. The Moslems were still masters of the kingdoms of Valencia, Murcia, Grenada, and Andalusia, with part of Algarva and the Balearic Isles, which last, until that time, had continued to be but little known to the Christians of the Continent.

These states were divided between several sovereigns, the principal of whom was Benhoud, a descendant of the ancient kings of Saragossa, a sagacious monarch and a great commander, who by his genius and courage had obtained dominion over all the southeastern part of Spain. Next to Benhoud in rank, the most important of these Mohammedan princes were the kings of Seville and Valentia. The barbarian who reigned at Majorca was a mere piratical chief, whose enmity was formidable only to the inhabitants of the neighbouring coast of Catalonia.

Such was the condition of Moorish Spain,

when two young heroes seated themselves, nearly at the same time, on the thrones of the two principal Christian states; and, after having allayed the commotions created during the period of their minority, directed their concentrated efforts against the Mussulmans, A.D. 1224, Heg. 621.

These princes, who were mutually desirous to emulate each other in fame, but were never rivals in interest, both consecrated their lives to the extirpation of the inflexible enemies of their native land. One of these sovereigns was Jacques I., king of Aragon (a son of the Peter of Aragon who distinguished himself on the field of Toloza), who united to the courage, grace, and energy of his father, a greater degree of genius and success than fell to the lot of that sovereign. The other was Ferdinand III., king of Castile and Leon, a discerning, courageous, and enterprising monarch, whom the Romish Church has numbered with its saints, and history ranks among its great men.

This prince was the nephew of Blanche of Castile, queen of France, and cousin-german of St. Lewis,* whom he nearly resembled in his

* See Note F, page 221.

piety, his bravery, and the wise laws he framed for the benefit of his subjects.

Ferdinand carried his arms first into Andalusia. When he entered the territories of the infidels, he received the homage of several Moorish princes, who came to acknowledge themselves his vassals. As he proceeded, he seized upon a great number of places, and, among others, the town of Alhambra, whose frightened inhabitants retired to Grenada, and established themselves in a portion of that city, which thus obtained the name by which it was afterward so much celebrated.

Jacques of Aragon, on his part, set sail with an army for the Balearic Isles. Though impeded in his progress by contrary winds, he succeeded at last in reaching Majorca, on the shore of which island he defeated the Moorish force that attempted to oppose his landing, and then marched towards their capital and laid siege to it.

The chivalrous Jacques, who, when danger was to be encountered, always took precedence of even his bravest officers and most daring soldiers, was, as usual, the first to mount the walls in the assault upon this city. It was carried, notwithstanding its great strength, the Mussulman king driven from the throne, and this new crown permanently incorporated with that of Aragon, A.D. 1229, Heg. 627.

Jacques had long been meditating a most important conquest. Valencia, after the death of the Cid, had again fallen into the hands of the Moors. This beautiful and fertile province, where nature seemed to delight herself by covering anew with fruit and flowers the soil that man had so often deluged with blood, was now under the dominion of Zeith, a brother of Mohammed El Nazir, the African king who was vanquished at Toloza by the Christians. A powerful faction, inimical to the power of Zeith, wished to place upon the throne a prince named Zean. The two competitors appealed to arms to decide their respective claims. The King of Aragon espoused the cause of Zeith, and, under pretext of marching to his assistance, advanced into the kingdom of Valencia, several times defeated Zean, seized upon his strong places, and, with the active intrepidity that rendered him so formidable a foe, invested the capital of his enemy, A.D. 1234, Heg. 632.

Thus pressed by the sovereign of Aragon,

Zean implored the aid of Benhoud, the most puissant of the kings of Andalusia. But Benhoud was at this time occupied in resisting the encroachments of Ferdinand. The Castilians, under the conduct of that valiant prince, had made new progress against the Moors. After possessing themselves of a great number of other cities, they had now laid siege to ancient Cordova.

Benhoud had been often vanquished, but always retained the affections of a people who regarded him as their last support. He had again collected an army, and, though possessed with an equally earnest desire to relieve both Cordova and Valencia, was about to march towards the latter, from a belief that he was most likely to be there successful, when his life was treacherously terminated by one of his lieutenants.

The Catholic kings were by this means delivered from the opposition of the only man who was capable of impeding the accomplishment of their wishes.

The death of Benhoud deprived the inhabitants of Cordova of all courage and hope. Until then they had defended themselves with equal courage and constancy; but they offered to capitulate upon receiving intelligence of this disastrous event.*

The Christians made the most rigorous use of their victory, granting only life and liberty of departure to the unfortunate disciples of the Prophet. An innumerable host of these wretched people came forth from their former homes, weeping, and despoiled of all their possessions. Slowly they left the superb city which had been for more than five hundred and twenty years the principal seat of their national greatness, their luxurious magnificence, their cherished religion, and their favourite literature and fine arts.

Often did these desolate exiles pause on their way, and turn their despairing eyes once again towards the towering palaces, the splendid temples, the beautiful gardens, that five centuries of lavish expense and toilsome effort had served to adorn and perfect, only to become the spoil of the enemies of their faith and their race.

The Catholic soldiers who were now the occupants of these enchanting abodes, were so far from appreciating their loveliness and value,

* A.D. 1236, Heg. 634.

that they preferred rather to destroy than inhabit them; and Ferdinand soon found himself the possessor of a deserted city. He was therefore compelled to attract inhabitants to Cordova from other parts of his dominions, by the offer of extraordinary immunities. But, notwithstanding the privileges thus accorded them, the Spaniards murmured at leaving their arid rocks and barren fields, to dwell in the palaces of caliphs and amid nature's most luxuriant scenes.

The grand mosque of Abderamus was converted into a cathedral, and Cordova became the residence of a bishop and canons, but it was never restored to the faintest shadow of its former splendour.

Not long after the fall of Cordova, Valencia also submitted to the Christian yoke. Zean, besides being assailed externally by the force of the intrepid Jacques, had, in addition, to oppose within his walls the faction of Zeith, whom he had dethroned. The king of Tunis, too, had been unsuccessful in an attempt to send a fleet to the relief of Valencia: it at once took to flight on the appearance of the vessels of Jacques. Abandoned by the whole world, disheartened by the fate of Cordova, and betrayed by the party of his competitor, Zean offered to become the vassal of the crown of Aragon, and to pay a tribute in acknowledgment of his vassalage; but the Christian monarch was inflexible, and would accede to no terms that did not include a stipulation to surrender the city.

Fifty thousand Moors, bearing their treasures with them, accompanied the departure of their sovereign from Valencia. Jacques had pledged his royal word to protect the rich booty which they so highly valued from the cupidity of his soldiers, and he faithfully performed his promise.

After the destruction of the two powerful kingdoms of Andalusia and Valencia, there seemed to exist no Moorish power capable of arresting the progress of the Spanish arms. That of Seville, which alone remained, was already menaced by the victorious Ferdinand. But, just at this period, a new state rose suddenly into importance, which maintained a high degree of celebrity for two hundred years, and long prevented the final ruin of the Moors.

FOURTH EPOCH.

THE KINGS OF GRENADA.

Extending from the middle of the Thirteenth Century to the period of the Total Expulsion of the Moors from Spain, A.D. 1492.

THE unprecedented success of the Spaniards, and, above all, the loss of Cordova, spread consternation among the Moors. That ardent and superstitious people, who were ever equally ready to cherish delusive hopes, and to yield to despondency when those anticipations were disappointed, looked upon their empire as ruined the moment the Christian cross surmounted the pinnacle of their grand mosque, and the banner of Castile waved over the walls of their ancient capital—those walls on which the standards of the Caliphs of the West and of their Prophet had for centuries floated in triumph.

Notwithstanding this national dejection, however, Seville, Grenada, Murcia, and the kingdom of Algarva still belonged to the Mussulmans. They possessed all the seaports, and the whole maritime coast of the south of Spain. Their enormous population, and great national wealth and industry, also secured to them immense resources; but Cordova, the holy city, the rival of Mecca in the West—Cordova was in the possession of the Christians, and the Moors believed that all was lost.

But the hopes of these despairing followers of Islam were rekindled by the almost magical influence of a single individual, a scion of the tribe of the *Alhamars*, named Mohammed Aboussaid, who came originally from the celebrated Arabian city of Couffa.

Several historians, who speak of Mohammed under the title of *Mohammed Alhamar*, assure us that he commenced his career as a simple shepherd, and that, having afterward borne arms, he aspired to the attainment of royal power in consequence of his martial exploits. Such an incident is not extraordinary among the Arabs, where all who are not descended either from the family of the Prophet or from the royal race, possessing none of the privileges of birth, are esteemed solely according to their personal merits.

But, be that as it may, Mohammed Aboussaid

possessed sufficient intellectual powers to reanimate the expiring courage of the vanquished Moslems. He assembled an army in the city of Arjona, and, well knowing the peculiar character of the nation that he wished to control, proceeded to gain over to his interests a *santon*, a species of religious character highly venerated among the Moors. This oracular individual publicly predicted to the people of Algarva that Mohammed Alhamar was destined speedily to become their king. Accordingly, he was soon proclaimed by the inhabitants, and several other cities followed the example thus set them.

Mohammed now filled the place of Benhoud, to whom he possessed similar talents for government; and, feeling the necessity of selecting a city to replace Cordova in the affections of the Moors, to become the sacred asylum of their religion, and the centring point for their military strength, he founded a new kingdom, and made the city of Grenada its capital, A.D. 1236, Heg 634.

This city, powerful from the remotest times, and supposed to be the ancient Illiberis of the Romans, was built upon two hills, not far distant from the Sierra Nevada, a chain of mountains whose summits are covered with perpetual snow. The town was traversed by the river Darra, and the waters of the Xenil bathed its walls. Each of the two hills was crowned by a fortress: on the one was that of the Alhambra, and on the other that of the Albayzin. These strongholds were either of them sufficient in extent to accommodate forty thousand men within their walls. The fugitives from the city of Alhambra, as has already been stated, had given the name of their former home to the new quarter that they peopled; and the Moors who had been driven from Baeca when Ferdinand III. became master of that place, had established themselves, in a similar manner, in the quarter of the Albayzin.

This city had also received many exiles from Valencia, Cordova, and other places which the Mussulmans had deserted.

With a population whose numbers were daily augmented, Grenada, at the period of which we now speak, was more than three leagues in circuit, surrounded by impregnable ramparts, defended by many strong towers, and by a brave and numerous people, whose military prowess seemed to ensure their safety and independence.

K

Various were the advantages that combined in giving to Grenada the supremacy she had assumed. Her location was one of the most agreeable and beautiful in the world, and rendered her mistress of a country on which nature had lavished her choicest gifts. The famous *vega*, or plain, by which the city was surrounded, was thirty leagues in length and eight in breadth. It was terminated on the north by the mountains of Elvira and the Sierra Nevada, and enclosed on the remaining sides by hills clothed with the verdure of the olive, the mulberry, the lemon, and the vine.

This enchanting plain was watered by five small rivers* and an infinite number of gushing springs, whose streams wandered in graceful meanderings through meadows of perpetual verdure, through forests of oak and plantations of grain, flax, and sugar-cane, or burst forth in the midst of gardens, and orchards, and orange-groves.

All the rich, and beautiful, and varied productions of the soil required but little attention in their culture. The earth was continually

* The Darra, Xenil, Dilar, Vagro, and Monachil.

covered with vegetation, in myriads of changing forms, and never knew the repose of winter.

During the heat of summer, the mountain breezes spread a refreshing coolness through the air of this lovely vega, and preserved the early brilliancy and beauty of the flowers, that were ever mingled in delightful confusion with the varied fruits of a tropical region.

On this celebrated plain, whose charms no description can embellish; on this enchanting vega, where nature seemed to have exhausted her efforts in lavishing all that the heart of man could desire or his imagination conceive, more blood has been shed than on any other spot in the world. There—where, during two centuries of unceasing warfare, whose baleful effects extended from generation to generation, from city to city, and from man to man—there does not exist a single isolated portion of earth where the trees have not been wantonly destroyed, the villages reduced to ashes, and the desolated fields strewn with the mingled corses of slaughtered Moors and Christians.

Independent of this *vega*, which was of such inestimable value to Grenada, fourteen great cities and more than one hundred of smaller size, together with a prodigious number of towns, were embraced within the boundaries of this fine kingdom.

The extent of Grenada, from Gibraltar (which was not taken by the Christians until long after this period) to the city of Lorca, was more than eighty leagues. It was thirty leagues in breadth from Cambril to the Mediterranean.

The mountains by which the kingdom of Grenada was intersected, produced gold, silver, granite, amethysts, and various kinds of marble.

Among these mountains, those of the Alpuxaries alone formed a province, and yielded the monarch of Grenada more precious treasures than their mines could furnish—active and athletic men, who became either hardy and industrious husbandmen, or faithful and indefatigable soldiers.

In addition to all this, the ports of Almeria, Malaga, and Algeziras received into their harbours the vessels of both Europe and Africa, and became places of deposite for the commerce of the Mediterranean and the Atlantic.

Such, at its birth, was the kingdom of Grenada, and such it long continued. Mohammed Alhamar, from the period of its establishment, made useless efforts to unite all the remaining dominions of the Mussulmans of Spain under one sceptre, as the only means of successfully resisting the encroachments of the Christians. But the little kingdom of Murcia and that of Algarva were each governed by separate princes, who persisted in maintaining their independence. This was the cause of their ruin, for they thus became more readily the prey of the Spaniards.

Alhamar signalized the commencement of his reign by military achievements. In the year 1242, Heg. 640, he gained some important advantages over the troops of Ferdinand. But repeated revolts in the capital and disturbances in other parts of his new empire, eventually compelled Mohammed to conclude a dishonourable peace with the King of Castile. He agreed to do homage for his crown to the Castilian sovereign, to put the strong place of Jaen into his hands, to pay him a tribute, and to furnish him with auxiliary troops for any wars in which he should engage. On these conditions Ferdinand acknowledged him King of Grenada, and even aided him in subduing his rebellious subjects.

The sagacious Ferdinand thus established a

truce with Grenada, that he might the more effectually concentrate his forces against Seville, which he had long entertained hopes of conquering.

The important city of Seville was no longer under the dominion of a king, but formed a kind of republic, governed by military magistrates. Its situation at no great distance from the mouth of the Guadalquivir, its commerce, its population, the mildness of the climate, and the fertility of the environs, rendered Seville one of the most flourishing cities of Spain.

Ferdinand, foreseeing a long resistance, commenced the campaign by seizing upon all the neighbouring towns.

Finally, he laid siege to Seville itself, and his fleet, stationed at the mouth of the Guadalquivir, closed the door to any assistance which might be sent from Africa in aid of the beleaguered city.

The siege was long and bloody. The Sevillians were numerous and well skilled in the arts of war, and their ally, the King of Algarva, harassed the besiegers unceasingly. Notwithstanding the extreme bravery displayed by the Christians in their assaults, and the scarcity of provisions which began to be felt within the walls, the city, after an investment of a whole year, still refused to surrender.

Ferdinand then summoned the King of Grenada to come, in accordance with their treaty, and serve under his banners. Alhamar was forced to obey, and soon presented himself in the Christian camp at the head of a brilliant army. The inhabitants of Seville lost all hope after this occurrence, and surrendered to the Castilian monarch. The King of Grenada returned to his own dominions with the humiliating glory of having contributed, by his assistance, to the ruin of his countrymen.

Ferdinand, with more piety than policy, banished the infidels from Seville. One hundred thousand of that unfortunate people left the city, to seek an exile's home in Africa or in the provinces of Grenada.

The kingdom of Grenada now became the sole and last asylum of the Spanish Moslems. The little kingdom of Algarva was soon obliged to receive the yoke of Portugal, and Murcia, in consequence of its separation from Grenada, became the prey of the Castilians.

During the life of Ferdinand III., nothing occurred to interrupt the good understanding that existed between that monarch and Mohammed Alhamar.

The King of Grenada wisely took advantage of this peaceful period more effectually to confirm himself in the possession of his crown, and to make preparations for a renewal of hostilities against the Christians, who would not, he foresaw, long remain his friends.

Mohammed, by this means, ultimately found himself in a condition that would enable him long to defend his power and dominions. He was master of a country of great extent, and he possessed considerable revenues, the amount of which it is now difficult correctly to estimate, in consequence of the ignorance which prevails on the subject of the peculiar financial system of the Moors, and the different sources from which the public treasury was supplied. Every husbandman, for example, paid the seventh part of the produce of his fields to his sovereign; his flocks even were not exempted from this exaction. The royal domain comprised numerous valuable farms; and, as agriculture was carried to the highest degree of perfection, the revenues from these, in so luxuriant a country, must have amounted to a very large sum. The annual income of the sovereign was augmented by various taxes levied on the sale, marking, and passage from one point to another of all kinds of cattle. The laws bestowed on the king the inheritance of such of his subjects as died childless, and gave him, in addition, a portion in the estates of other deceased persons. He also possessed, as has been already shown, mines of gold, silver, and precious stones; and though the Moors were but little skilled in the art of mining, still there was no country in Europe in which gold and silver were more common than among them.

The commerce carried on in their beautiful silks, and in a great variety of other productions; their contiguity to the Mediterranean and Atlantic; their activity, industry, and astonishing population; their superior knowledge of the science of agriculture; the sobriety natural to all the inhabitants of Spain; and that peculiar property of a southern climate, by which much is produced from the soil, while very little suffices for the maintenance of its possessor; all these, united with their other national advantages, will furnish some idea of the great power and resources of this singular people.

Their standing military force—it can scarcely be said in times of peace, for they rarely knew the blessings of that state—amounted to nearly a hundred thousand men; and this army, in case of necessity, could easily be increased to double that number. The single city of Grenada could furnish fifty thousand soldiers. Indeed, every Moor would readily become a soldier to oppose the Christians. The difference of faith rendered these wars sacred in their eyes; and the mutual hatred entertained by these two almost equally superstitious nations never failed to arm, when necessary, every individual of both sides, even from children to old men.

Independent of the numerous and brave, but ill-disciplined troops, who would assemble for a campaign, and afterward return to their homes without occasioning any expense to the state, the Moorish monarch maintained a considerable corps of cavaliers, who were dispersed along the frontiers, particularly in the directions of Murcia and Jaen, those parts of the country being most exposed to the repeated incursions of the Spaniards. Upon each of these cavaliers the king bestowed for life a small habitation, with sufficient adjoining ground for his own maintenance, and that of his family and horse. This method of keeping soldiers in service, while it occasioned no expense to the public treasury, served to attach them more firmly to their country, by identifying their interests with hers; and it held out to them the strongest motives faithfully to defend their charge, inasmuch as their patrimony was always first exposed to the ravages of the enemy.

At a time when the art of war had not reached the perfection it has now attained, and when large bodies of troops were not kept continually assembled and exercised, the system of stationing this peculiar guard along the frontiers was of admirable effect.

The knights who composed this unrivalled cavalry were mounted on African or Andalusian chargers, whose merits in the field are so well-known, and were accustomed from infancy to their management; treating them with the tenderest care, and regarding them as their inseparable companions: by these means they acquired that remarkable superiority for which the Moorish cavalry is still so celebrated.

These redoubtable squadrons, whose velocity of movement was unequalled; who would, almost at the same moment, charge in mass, break into detached troops, scatter, rally, fly off, and again form in line; these cavaliers, whose voice, whose slightest gesture, whose very thoughts, so to speak, were intelligible to their docile and sagacious steeds, and who were able to recover a lance or sabre that had fallen to the earth while in full gallop, constituted the principal military force of the Moors. Their infantry was of little value; and their ill-fortified towns, surrounded only by walls and moats, and defended by this worthless infantry, could offer but an imperfect resistance to that of the Spaniards, which began already to deserve the reputation it afterward so well sustained in Italy, under Gonzalvo, the Great Captain.

After the death of St. Ferdinand, his son Alphonso the Sage* mounted the throne, A.D. 1252, Heg. 650. The first care of Mohammed Alhamar after this event was to go in person to Toledo, followed by a brilliant retinue, to renew the treaty of alliance, or, rather, of dependance, by which he was united to Ferdinand

* See note A, page 222

The new king of Castile remitted on this occasion a part of the tribute to which the Moors had been subjected.

But this peace was not of long continuance; and the two contending nations now recommenced the war with nearly equal advantages.

An incident is related as having occurred during this war, which reflects equal honour on the humanity of the Moors and the courage of the Spaniards. It refers to Garcias Gomes, governor of the city of Xeres. He was besieged by the Grenadians, and his garrison nearly destroyed, but still he refused to surrender; and, standing on the ramparts covered with blood, and literally bristling with arrows, he sustained alone the onset of the assailants. The Moors, on seeing him in this situation, agreed, with one accord, to spare the life of so brave a man. Garcias then threw himself from the walls upon some iron hooks; but he was rescued alive in spite of his efforts to prevent it, treated with respect by his captors, and, after his wounds were healed, dismissed with presents.

Alhamar could not prevent Alphonso from adding the kingdom of Murcia to his dominions; and the fortunes of war compelled him to obtain peace by submitting anew to the payment of tribute to the Catholic sovereign, A.D. 1266, Heg. 665.

But some dissensions which soon after arose between the Castilian monarch and some of the grandees of his kingdom, inspired the Grenadian king with the hope of repairing the loss he had sustained. The brother of Alphonso, together with several noblemen belonging to the principal Castilian families, retired to Grenada in open defiance of the authority of the Spanish monarch, and materially aided Mohammed Alhamar in repressing the insurrectionary movements of two of his rebellious subjects, who were countenanced in their attempts by the Christians.

But, just at this juncture, the wise and politic King of Grenada died, leaving the throne that he had acquired and preserved by his talents to his son Mohammed II., El Fakik, A.D. 1273, Heg. 672.

The new Mussulman king, who took the title of *Emir al Mumenim*, adopted in all respects the policy of his father. He took every advantage in his power of the discord which reigned at the Castilian court, and of the ineffectual voyages undertaken by Alphonso in the hope of being elected emperor.* Finally, during the absence of his enemy, Mohammed formed an offensive league with Jacob, the king of Morocco, a prince of the race of the *Merines*, the conquerors and successors of the Almohades. The Grenadian sovereign ceded to his African ally the two important places of Tariffe and Algeziras, on condition of his crossing the Mediterranean to the Peninsula.

Jacob, in accordance with this agreement, arrived in Spain, at the head of an army, in the year 1275 (the 675th of the Hegira); and the two Moorish leaders, by acting in concert, gained some important advantages.

But the criminal revolt of Sancho, the Infant of Castile, against his father Alphonso the Sage, soon afterward divided these Mussulman monarchs. The King of Grenada took the part of the rebellious son, while Alphonso, reduced to extremity by the abandonment of his subjects, implored the assistance of the King of Morocco. Jacob recrossed the sea with his troops, and met Alphonso at Zara. At that celebrated interview, the unfortunate Castilian wished to concede the place of honour to the king, who was there as

* See note B, page 222.

his defender. "It belongs to you," said Jacob to him, "because you are unfortunate! I came here to avenge a cause which should be that of every father. I came here to aid you in punishing an ingrate, who, though he received life from you, would still deprive you of your crown. When I shall have fulfilled this duty, and you are again prosperous and happy, I will once more become your enemy, and contest every point of precedence with you."

The soul of the Christian prince was not sufficiently noble, however, to prompt him to confide himself to the monarch who had uttered these sentiments, and he escaped from the camp. Alphonso died soon after this event, disinheriting his guilty son before he expired, A.D. 1284, Heg. 683.

Sancho* reigned in his father's stead, however, notwithstanding this prohibition, and international troubles convulsed Castile anew.

Mohammed seized this moment to enter Andalusia. He gained several battles, and took some important places in that kingdom, and thus victoriously terminated a long and glorious reign, A.D. 1302, Heg. 703.

* See note C, page 222.

This Mohammed *Emir al Mumenim*, the principal political events of whose life have now been briefly narrated, was a munificent patron of the fine arts. He added their charms to the attractions of a court which poets, philosophers, and astronomers alike contributed to render celebrated.

As an illustration of the scientific superiority that the Moors still maintained over the Spaniards, the fact may be mentioned that Alphonso the Sage, king of Castile, availed himself, in the arrangement of his astronomical tables (still known as the *Alphonsine Tables*), of the assistance of some contemporary Moslem *savans*.

Grenada began by this time to replace Cordova. Architecture, above all, made great advances. It was during the reign of Mohammed II. that the famous palace of the Alhambra was commenced, a part of which still remains to astonish travellers, whom its name alone suffices to attract to Grenada.

To prove to what a height of perfection the Moors had succeeded in carrying the art, then so little known to Europeans, of uniting the magnificent and the luxurious, a few details may perhaps be pardoned concerning this singular edifice, and as an illustration, also, of the particular manners and customs of the Moors.

The Alhambra, as has been said, was at first only a vast fortress, standing upon one of the two hills enclosed within the city of Grenada. This hill, though environed on every side by the waters either of the Darra or the Xenil, was defended, in addition, by a double enclosure of walls. It was on the summit of this elevation, which overlooked the whole city, and from which one might behold the most beautiful prospect in the world, in the midst of an esplanade covered with trees and fountains, that Mohammed selected the site of his palace.

Nothing with which we are familiar in architecture can give us a correct idea of that of the Moors. They piled up buildings without order, symmetry, or any attention to the external appearance they would present. All their cares were bestowed upon the interior of their structures. There they exhausted all the resources of taste and magnificence, to combine in their apartments the requisites for luxurious indulgence with the charms of nature in her most enchanting forms. There, in saloons adorned with the most beautiful marble, and paved with a brilliant imitation of porcelain, couches, covered with stuffs of gold or silver, were arranged near *jets d'eau,* whose waters glanced upward towards the vaulted roof, and spread a delicious coolness through an atmosphere embalmed by the delicate odours arising from exquisite vases of precious perfumes, mingled with the fragrant breath of the myrtle, jasmine, orange, and other sweet-scented flowers that adorned the apartments.

The beautiful palace of the Alhambra, as it now exists at Grenada,* presents no *façade.* It is approached through a charming avenue, which is constantly intersected by rivulets, whose streams wander in graceful curves amid groups of trees. The entrance is through a large square tower, which formerly bore the name of the *Hall of Judgment.* A religious inscription announces that it was there that the king administered justice after the ancient manner of the Hebrew and other Oriental nations. Several buildings,

* It should be borne in mind, that the description given by M. Florian of the remains of the once gorgeous splendours of this palace was written nearly half a century ago ; and that time, and the yet more ruthless destroyer man, may have wrought great changes since that period and the ruins of the Alhambra.—*Trans.*

which once adjoined this tower were destroyed in more recent times, to give place to a magnificent palace erected by Charles V., a description of which is not necessary to our subject. Upon penetrating on the northern side into the ancient palace of the Moorish kings, one feels as if suddenly transported to the regions of fairyland. The first court is an oblong square, surrounded on each side by a gallery in the form of an arcade, the walls and ceiling of which are covered with Mosaic work, festoons, arabesque paintings, gilding, and carving in stucco, of the most admirable workmanship. All the plain spaces between these various ornaments are filled with passages transcribed from the Alkoran, or by inscriptions of a similar character to the following, which will suffice to create some idea of the figurative style of Moorish composition.

"Oh Nazir! thou wert born the master of a throne, and, like the star that announces the approach of day, thou art refulgent with a brilliancy that belongs to thee alone! Thine arm is the rampart of a nation; thy justice an all-pervading luminary. Thou canst, by thy valour, subdue those who have given companions to

God! Thy numerous people are thy children, and thou renderest them all happy by thy goodness. The bright stars of the firmament shine lovingly upon thee, and the glorious light of the sun beams upon thee with affection. The stately cedar, the proud monarch of the forest, bows his lofty head at thy approach, and is again uplifted by thy puissant hand!"

In the midst of this court, which is paved with white marble, is a long basin always filled with running water of sufficient depth for bathing. It is bordered on each side by beds of flowers, and surrounded by walks lined with orange-trees. The place was called the *Mesuar*, and served as the common bathing-place of those who were attached to the service of the palace.

From thence one passes into the celebrated *Court of Lions*. It is a hundred feet in length and fifty in breadth. A colonnade of white marble supports the gallery that runs around the whole. These columns, standing sometimes two and sometimes three together, are of slender proportions and fantastic design; but their lightness and grace afford pleasure to the eye of the wondering beholder. The walls, and, above all, the ceiling of the circular gallery, are covered with embellishments of gold, azure, and stucco, wrought into arabesques, with an exquisite delicacy of execution that the most skilful modern workmen would find it difficult to rival. In the midst of these ornaments of ever-changing variety and beauty are inscribed passages from the Koran, such as the following, which all good Mussulmans are required frequently to repeat: *God is great: God alone is supreme: There is no god but God: Celestial enjoyment, gratifications of the heart, delights of the soul to all those who believe.*

At either extremity of the Court of Lions are placed, within the interior space enclosed by the gallery, and, like it, supported by marble columns, two elegant cupolas of fifteen or sixteen feet in circumference. These graceful domes form a covering for beautiful *jets d'eau.* In the centre of the lengthened square, a superb alabaster vase, six feet in diameter, is supported in an elevated position in the midst of a vast basin by the forms of twelve lions sculptured from white marble. This vessel, which is believed to have been modelled after the design of the "molten sea" of the Temple of Solomon, is again surmounted by a smaller vase, from which shoot forth innumerable tiny cascades, which together present the form of a great sheaf; and, falling again from one vase into another, and from these into the large basin beneath, create a perpetual flow, whose volume is increased by the floods of limpid water which gush in a continual stream from the mouth of each of the marble lions.

This fountain, like each of the others, is adorned with inscriptions; for the Moors ever took pleasure in mingling the eloquence of poetry with the graces of sculpture. To us their conceptions appear singular and their expressions exaggerated; but our manners are so opposite to theirs; the period of their existence as a nation is so far removed, and we know so little of the genius of their language, that we have, perhaps, no right to judge the literature of the Moors by the severe rules of modern criticism. And, indeed, the specimens we possess of the French and Spanish poetry of the thirteenth and fourteenth centuries are, many of them, little superior to the verses engraven on the Fountain of Lions, of which the following is a translation.*

* The translator has adopted the *literal* French version of this inscription, given in a note by M. Florian, from the impression that the spirit of the original would thus be better

"Oh thou who beholdest these lions! dost thou not perceive that they need only to breathe to possess the perfection of nature? Oh Mohammed! Oh potent sovereign! God originated and prolonged thy existence, that thou mightest be inspired with the genius to conceive and accomplish these novel and beautiful embellishments! Thy soul is adorned by the most ennobling qualities of humanity. This enchanting spot pictures thy admirable virtues. Like the lion, thou art terrible in combat; and nothing can be more justly compared to the bountiful and unceasing profusion of the limpid waters which gush from the bosom of this fountain, and fill the air with glittering and brilliant particles, than the liberal hand of Mohammed."

We will not attempt a description in detail of such other portions of the palace of the Alhambra as still exist. Some of these served as halls of audience or of justice; others enclosed the baths of the king, the queen, and their children Sleeping apartments still remain, where the couches were disposed either in alcoves, or upon platforms covered with the peculiar pavement

preserved than by attempting to render into rhyme his poetical interpretation.

already alluded to; but always near a fountain, the unceasing murmur of whose dreamy voice might sooth the occupants to repose.

In the music saloon of this once luxurious royal abode are four elevated galleries, which, ere the glory of the Alhambra had passed away, were often filled by Moorish musicians, the delightful strains of whose varied instruments enchanted the court of Grenada. Then the fair and the brave reclined in graceful groups in the centre of the apartment, upon rich Oriental carpets, surrounding the alabaster fountain, whose balmy breath diffused refreshing coolness, and whose softly gurgling sounds mingled with the gentle music which was ever the accompaniment of repose and enjoyment.

In an apartment which was at the same time the oratory and dressing-room of the queen of this magnificent residence, there still exists a slab of marble, pierced with an infinite number of small apertures, to admit the exhalations of the perfumes that were incessantly burning beneath the lofty ceiling. From this part of the palace, too, the views are exquisitely beautiful. The windows and doors opening from it are so arranged, that the most agreeable prospects, the

M

mellowest and most pleasing effects of light, perpetually fall upon the delighted eyes of those within, while balmy breezes constantly renew the delicious coolness of the air that breathes through this enchanting retreat.

Upon leaving the marble halls and lofty towers of the Alhambra, one discerns, on the side of a neighbouring mountain, the famous garden of the *Generalif*, which signifies, in the Moorish tongue, the *Home of Love*. In this garden was the palace to which the kings of Grenada repaired to pass the season of spring. It was built in a style similar to that of the Alhambra: the same gorgeous splendour, the same costly magnificence reigned there. The edifice is now destroyed; but the picturesque situation, the ever-varied and ever-charming landscape, the limpid fountains, the sparkling *jets d'eau*, and tumbling waterfalls of the *Generalif*, are still left to excite admiration.

The terraces of this garden are in the form of an amphitheatre, and the lingering remains of their once beautiful Mosaic pavements are still to be seen. The walks are now darkly umbrageous, from the interwoven branches of gigantic cypresses and aged myrtles, beneath whose gratefu shades the kings and queens of Grenada have so often wandered. Then blooming groves and forests of fruit-trees were agreeably intermingled with graceful domes and marble pavilions: then the sweet perfume of the countless flowers that mingled their varied dyes in delightful confusion, floated in the soft air. Then the delicate tendrils of the vine clasped the supporting branches of the orange, and both together hung the mingled gold and purple of their clustering fruits over the bright waters that from marble founts

"Gushed up to sun and air!"

Then valour and beauty strayed side by side, beneath embowering branches, the fire of the one attempered to gentleness by the softer graces of the other, and the souls of both elevated and purified by nature's holy and resistless influences.

But now the luxuriant vine lies prostrate, its climbing trunk and clinging tendrils rudely torn from their once firm support: even the voice of the fountain no longer warbles in the same gladsome tone as of yore; the mouldering fragments of the polished column and sculptured dome are now strewed on the earth; the sighing of the gentle breeze no longer awakens the soft breath of responding flowers; the loveliness and the glory of the *Home of Love* are vanished away for ever; and the crumbling stones of the tesselated pavements echo naught but the lingering footfall of the solitary stranger, who wanders thither to enjoy those mournful charms of which the destroyer cannot divest a spot that must ever appeal so strongly to the vision and the heart, to the memory and the imagination.

It is painful to quit the Alhambra and the Generalif, to return to the ravages, incursions, and sanguinary quarrels of the Moors and Christians.

It was the fate of Mohammed III. (surnamed the Blind) to be obliged at the same time to repress the rebellious movements of his own subjects and repel the invasions of his Catholic neighbours. Compelled by the infirmity from which he derived his appellation to choose a prime minister, he bestowed that important post upon Farady, the husband of his sister, a judicious statesman and a brave soldier, who for some time prosperously continued the war against the Castilians, and finally concluded it by an honourable peace.

But the courtiers, jealous of the glory and envious of the good-fortune of the favourite, formed a conspiracy against his master, and instigated revolts among the people. To complete his calamities, foreign war again broke forth; the King of Castile, Ferdinand IV., surnamed *the Summoned*,* united with the King of Aragon in attacking the Grenadians.†

Gibraltar was taken by the Castilians, and the conqueror expelled its Moorish inhabitants from its walls. Among the unfortunate exiles who departed from the city was an old man, who, perceiving Ferdinand, approached him, leaning on his staff: "King of Castile," he said to him, "what injury have I done to thee or thine? Thy great-grandfather Ferdinand drove me from my native Seville: I sought an asylum at Xeres; thy grandfather Alphonso banished me from thence: retiring within the walls of Tariffe,‡ thy father Sancho exiled me from that city. At last I came to find a grave at the extremity of Spain, on the shore of Gibraltar; but thy hatred hath pursued me even here: tell me now of one place on earth where I can die unmolested by the Christians!"

* See Note D, page 223.   † A.D. 1302, Heg. 703.
‡ See note E, page 224.

"Cross the sea!" replied the Spanish prince; and he caused the aged petitioner to be conveyed to Africa.

Vanquished by the Aragonians, harassed by the Castilians, and alarmed by the seditious proceedings which the grandees of his court were encouraging among his own subjects, the King of Grenada and his prime minister were forced to conclude a shameful peace.

The intestine storm, whose gathering had long disturbed the domestic security of the kingdom, soon after burst forth. Mohammed Abenazar, brother to Mohammed the Blind, and the head of the conspiracy, seized the unfortunate monarch, put him to death, and assumed his place, A.D. 1310, Heg. 710.

But the usurper himself was soon driven from his throne by Farady, the ancient minister, who, not daring to appropriate the crown to himself, placed it on the head of his son Ismael, the nephew of Mohammed the Blind, through his mother, the sister of that monarch.

This event took place A.D. 1313, Heg. 713. From that period the royal family of Grenada was divided into two branches, which were ever after at enmity with each other; the one, called the *Alhamar*, included the descendants of the first king through the males of the line, and the other, named *Farady*, was that of such of his offspring as were the children of the female branches of the royal race.

The Castilians, whose interests were always promoted by cherishing dissensions among their Moorish neighbours, lent their countenance to Abenazar, who had taken refuge in the city of Grenada. The Infant Don Pedro, uncle to the youthful King of Castile, Alphonso *the Avenger*, as he was surnamed, took the field against Ismael, and several times gave battle to the followers of the Crescent. Then joining his forces to those of another Infant named Don Juan, the two friends carried fire and sword to the very ramparts of Grenada. The infidel warriors did not venture to sally from their walls to repel the invaders; but when, loaded with booty, the Christians had commenced their return to Castile, Ismael followed on their route with his army, and, soon overtaking his ruthless foes, fell suddenly upon their rear. It was now the 26th of June,* and the time chosen by the Mussulmans for the attack was the hottest hour of a

* A.D. 1319, Heg. 719.

burning day. The two Spanish princes made such violent efforts to reorganize their scattered bands and to recover their lost authority, that, exhausted at last by thirst and fatigue, they both fell dead without having received a wound.

The dismayed and exhausted Spaniards could now no longer offer any resistance to their furious enemies. They betook themselves to flight, leaving their baggage, with the bodies of the two unfortunate Infants, on the field of battle. Ismael caused the remains of these princes to be conveyed to Grenada and deposited in coffins covered with cloth of gold: he then restored them to the Castilians, after having bestowed on them the most distinguished funeral honours.*

This victory was rapidly followed by the conquest of several cities and the establishment of an honourable truce. But Ismael did not live to enjoy the fruits of his success: being enamoured of a young Spanish captive, who had fallen, in the division of the spoils, to the share of one of his officers, the king so far forgot the laws of justice and honour as to possess himself

* The mountains of Grenada, in the neighbourhood of which this action took place, have, ever since that event, borne the name of LA SIERRA DE LOS INFANTES.

by force of the beautiful slave. Such an insult among the followers of Islam can only be expiated by blood: the monarch was assassinated by his exasperated officer. His son Mohammed V. mounted the throne in his stead, A.D. 1322, Heg. 722.

The reign of Mohammed V. and that of his successor Joseph I., both of whom perished in the same manner (being murdered in their palace), present nothing during thirty years but an unbroken series of ravages, seditions, and combats.

At the request of the Grenadians, Abil-Hassan, king of Morocco, of the dynasty of the *Merinis*, landed in Spain at the head of innumerable troops, with whom he joined the army of Joseph. The kings of Castile and Portugal unitedly gave battle to this immense army on the shores of Salado, not far from the city of Tariffe. This encounter, equally celebrated with the victory of Toloza in the history of Spain, terminated in the defeat of the Moors. Abil-Hassan returned hastily to Morocco, to conceal within his own dominions his chagrin at its unexpected and disastrous issue.

The strong place of Algeziras, the bulwark of

Grenada, and the magazine in which was deposited the necessary supplies received by that kingdom from Africa, was besieged by the Castilians A.D. 1342, Heg. 742. Several French, English, and Navarrois cavaliers resorted on this occasion to the camp of the beleaguering army. The Mussulmans availed themselves of the use of cannon in the defence of their city; and this is the first time that the employment of that description of ordnance is spoken of in history. We are told that it was used at the battle of Cressy by the English; but that event did not take place until four years after the date of the present siege. It is, then, to the Spanish Moors that we owe, not the discovery of gunpowder (for that is attributed by some to the Chinese, by others to a German monk named Schwartz, and by others again to Roger Bacon, an Englishman), but the terrible invention of artillery. It is at least certain, that the Moors planted the first cannon of which we have any account. But, in spite of the advantages it thus possessed, Algeziras was taken by the Christians, A.D. 1344, Heg. 745.

About ten years after this event, the unfortunate Joseph, who had been so often attacked by foreign enemies, met his death from the hands of his own subjects.

It may have been remarked by the reader, that no established law regulated the regal succession among the Moors. Yet, notwithstanding the perpetual conspiracies and intrigues which rendered the possession of the crown so insecure and of such uncertain duration, a prince of the royal race always occupied the throne. We have seen Grenada divided, since the violent termination of the reign of Ismael, between the factions of the *Alhamar* and the *Farady*, and the former deposed by the latter, who always regarded the Alhamars as usurpers. This unhappy contest was the source of numberless disorders, conspiracies, and assassinations.

The monarch next in order to Joseph I. on the throne of Grenada was his uncle, a Farady prince named Mohammed VI., and called *the Old*, in consequence of his succeeding at a somewhat advanced period of life.

Mohammed the Red, a scion of the Alhamar race, drove his cousin, Mohammed the Old, from the throne, A.D. 1360, Heg. 762, and retained it for some years, through the protection of the King of Aragon.

Peter the Cruel, then king of Castile, espoused the cause of the banished Farady, supported his claims by warlike arguments, and so closely pressed Mohammed the Alhamar, that he adopted the resolution of repairing to Seville, and abandoning himself to the magnanimity of his royal foe.

Mohammed arrived at the court of Seville accompanied by a suite composed of his most faithful friends, and bearing with him vast treasures. He presented himself with noble confidence in the presence of the monarch. "King of Castile!" said he to Peter, "the blood alike of Christian and Moor has too long flowed in my contest with the Farady. You protect my rival; yet it is you whom I select to adjudge our quarrel. Examine my claims and those of my enemy, and pronounce who shall be the sovereign of Grenada. If you decide in favour of the Farady, I demand only to be conducted to Africa; if you accord the preference to me, receive the homage that I have come to render you for my crown!"

The astonished Peter lavished honours upon the Mussulman king, and caused him to be seated at his side during the magnificent feast by which he signalized the occasion. But, when the Alhamar retired from the entertainment, he was seized and thrown into prison. From thence he was afterward conducted through the streets of the city, seated, half naked, upon an ass, and led to a field termed the *Tablada*, where thirty-seven of his devoted followers were deprived of their heads in his presence. The execrable Peter, envying the executioner the pleasure of shedding his blood, then thrust through the unfortunate King of Grenada with his own lance. The dying sovereign uttered only these words as he expired, "Oh Peter, Peter, what a deed for a cavalier!"

By a very extraordinary fatality, every throne in Spain was at this period occupied by princes whose characters were blackened by the most atrocious crimes. Peter the Cruel, the Nero of Castile, assassinated the kings who confided themselves to his protection, put to death his wife Blanche of Bourbon, and, in short, daily imbrued his hands in the blood of his relatives or friends. Peter IV. of Aragon, less violent than the Castilian, but equally unfeeling and even more perfidious, despoiled one of his brothers of his kingdom, commanded another to be put to death, and delivered his ancient preceptor to the executioners. Peter I., king of Portugal, the lover of the celebrated Inez de Castro,* whose ferocity was doubtless excited and increased by the cruelty that had been exercised against his mistress, tore out the hearts of the murderers of Inez, and poisoned a sister with whom he was displeased. Finally, the contemporary King of Navarre was that Charles the Bad, whose name alone is sufficient still to cause a shudder. All Spain groaned beneath the iron rule of these monsters of cruelty, and was inundated by the blood of their victims. If it be remembered that, at the same time, France had become a prey to the horrors which followed the imprisonment of King John; that England witnessed the commencement of the troubled reign of Richard II.; that Italy was delivered up to the contentions of the rival factions of the Guelfs and Ghibelines, and beheld two occupants at the same time upon the papal throne; that two emperors disputed the right to the imperial crown of Germany; and that Timurlane ravaged Asia from the territories of the Usbeks to the borders of India, it will not be disputed

* See Note F, page 224.

that the history of the world records the annals of no more unhappy epoch in its affairs.

Grenada was at last tranquil after the crime of Peter the Cruel. Mohammed the Old, or the Farady, being now freed from the rival claims of his competitor, remounted the throne without opposition.

Mohammed was the only ally of the King of Castile who remained faithful to that inhuman monster up to the period of his death. Peter was at last the victim of a crime similar to those of which he had so often himself been guilty: his illegitimate brother, Henry de Transtamare, deprived him of his crown and his life, A.D. 1369, Heg. 771.

The King of Grenada made peace with the new sovereign of Castile, maintained it for several years, and finally left his kingdom in a flourishing condition to his son Mohammed VIII., Abouhadjad, called by the Spanish historians Mohammed Gaudix.

This prince commenced his reign A.D. 1379, Heg. 782. He was the best and wisest of the Spanish Mohammedan kings. Intent only upon promoting the happiness of his people, he was desirous of securing to them the enjoyment of that foreign and domestic peace to which they had so long been almost utter strangers. The more effectually to ensure this, Abouhadjad commenced his reign with fortifying his towns, raising a strong army, and allying himself with the King of Tunis, whose daughter Cadiga he espoused. When well prepared for war, the Moorish sovereign sent ambassadors to the King of Castile, to solicit his friendship. Don Juan, the son and successor of Henry de Transtamare, being sufficiently occupied by his quarrels with Portugal and England, readily signed a treaty with the royal follower of the Crescent; and Abouhadjad, on his part, kept it unbroken. Secured from the inroads of the Christians, this wise monarch now occupied himself in promoting the increase of agriculture and commerce: he likewise diminished the rates of imposts, and soon found his income increased in consequence of this judicious measure. Beloved by a people whom he rendered happy, respected by foreign neighbours whom he had no reason to fear, and possessed of an amiable wife, who alone engaged his affections, this excellent Mussulman prince spent the wealth and leisure that he could with propriety devote to such objects, in adorning his capital, in cherishing the fine arts, and in cultivating architecture and poetry. Several monuments of his munificence existed at Grenada, and at Gaudix, a city in favour of which he entertained strong predilections. His court was the favoured abode of genius and elegance.

The Moors of Spain still possessed poets, physicians, painters, sculptors, academies, and universities. And these were all liberally encouraged and endowed by Mohammed Gaudix.

Most of the productions of the Grenadian authors of this period perished at the final conquest of their country;* but some of them have been preserved, and still exist in the library of the Escurial. They chiefly treat of grammar, astrology (then greatly esteemed), and, above all, of theology, a study in which the Moors excelled. That people, naturally gifted with discriminating minds and ardent imaginations, produced many distinguished theologians, who may easily be supposed to have introduced into Europe the unfortunate scholastic taste for subtle questions and disputes, which once rendered so celebrated, men whose names and achievements have since sunk for ever into oblivion. The pre-

* See Note G, page 225.

tended secrets of the cabal, of alchymy, of judicial astronomy, of the divining rod, and all the accounts, formerly so common, of sorcerers, magicians, and enchanters, are derived from these descendants of the Arabs. They were a superstitious race from the remotest times; and it is probable that to their residence in Spain, and their long intercourse with the Spaniards, is owing that love for the marvellous, and that well-deserved reputation for superstitious credulity, with which philosophy still reproaches a sprightly and intellectual nation, upon whom nature has bestowed the germes of the best qualities that adorn humanity.

A kind of literature which was common among these Saracens, and for which the Spaniards were indebted to them, was that of novels or romances. The Arabs were ever, as they still are, passionate lovers of story-telling. As well in the tents of the wild Bedouin as in the palaces of the East, alike under the gilded domes and peasant roofs of Grenada, this taste prevailed. Everywhere they assembled nightly to listen to romantic narratives of love and valour. Everywhere they listened in silent attention, or wept from sympathetic interest in the fate of those whose adventures formed the subject of the tale. The Grenadians joined with this passion for exciting incident, a taste for music and singing. Their poets imbodied in verse these favourite recitals of love and war. Musicians were employed in composing suitable airs for them, and they were thus sung by the youthful Moors with all the enthusiasm that passion, poetry, and dulcet harmony can unitedly inspire. From this national custom are derived the multitude of Spanish romances, translated or imitated from the Arabic, which, in a simple and sometimes touching style, recount the fierce combats of the Moors and Christians, the fatal quarrels of jealous and haughty rivals, or the tender conversation of lovers. They describe with great exactness everything relating to the peculiar manners and amusements of this interesting and extinguished nation: their fêtes, their games of the ring and of canes, and their bull-fights, the latter of which they adopted from the Spaniards, are all portrayed. Thus we learn that their warlike equipments consisted of a large cimeter, a slender lance, a short coat of mail, and a light leathern buckler. We have descriptions of superb horses, with their richly-jewelled and embroidered housings sweeping the earth in ample folds, and of the devises emblazoned on the arms of the graceful Moorish cavaliers. These last consisted frequently of a heart pierced by an arrow, or perhaps of a star guiding a vessel, or of the first letter of the name of the fair recipients of their vows of love. We learn, too, that their colours each bore a peculiar signification: yellow and black expressed grief; green, hope; blue, jealousy; violet and flame colour, passionate love.

The following abridged translation of one of these little compositions will produce a more correct idea of them in the mind of the reader than any description could convey.*

GONZULO AND ZELINDA.

A MOORISH ROMANCE.

In a transport of jealousy and pride,
Zelinda spurned her lover from her side !

---

* The translator ventures to offer an imitation of M. Florian's French version of this Moorish ballad, and appends the *Spanish* original with which he presents his readers.

GANZUL Y ZELINDA.

ROMANCE MORO.

En el tiempo que Zelinda
Cerro ayrada la ventana

His cruel doom Gonzulo heard
With bosom wrung; and disappeared!
But the fair maid soon deeply felt
The torturing wound herself had dealt;
As glides the snow from mountain crest,
So fled resentment from her breast.

They tell her that the Moor's proud heart
Is pierced by grief's most poisoned dart,
And that he'd doffed, when flying from her side,
The tender colours that were once his pride;
That green, of hope the cherished emblem gay,
To sorrow's mournful hues had given way.
A badge of crape his lance's point now wears,
A blackened crown his shield as emblem bears!

A la disculpa a los zelos
Que el Moro Ganzul le daya,
Confusa y arrepentida
De averse fingido ayrada,
Por verle y desagravialle,
El corazon se le abraza;
Que en el villano de amor
Es mui cierta la mudanza, etc.

Y como supo que el Moro
Rompio furioso la lanca, etc.
Y que la librea verde
Avia trocado en leonada;
Saco luego una marlota
De tufetan roxo y plata,
Un bizarro capellar
De tela de oro morada, etc.

To proffer gifts with different meaning fraught,
Zelinda now her errant lover sought:
The blue of jealousy she had united
With all the hues most dear to lovers plighted ;
A violet gem, entwined with gold,
Gleamed mid a broidered turban's fold;
And every silken riband that she bore,
Of lovely innocence the symbol wore.

Zelinda reached the soft retreat
Where Gonzulo his fate must meet!
O'erwhelmed with doubt, the dark-eyed maid
Reclined beneath a myrtle shade,
And sent a faithful page to guide
Her banished lover to her side.
Gonzulo scarce the message would receive,
For wo had taught his heart to disbelieve!

Con une bonete cubierto
De zaphires y esparaldas,
Que publican zelos muertos,
Y vivas las esperancos,
Con una nevada toça;
Que el color de la veleta
Tambien publica bononça
Informandose primero.

A donde Ganzul estava,
A una caza de plazer
Aquella tarde le llama;
Y diziendole a Ganzul
Que Zelinda le aguardava,
Al page le pregunto

But soon he flew, on wing of love,
To seek Zelinda's chosen grove.
Then tearful glances of regret
By words of tenderness were met;
And ne'er did guardian nymphs record
More ardent vows than there were poured!
'Twas thus triumphant love repaired
The cruel wrongs that each had shared!

The delicate and peculiar gallantry, which rendered the Moors of Grenada famous throughout Europe, formed a singular contrast to the ferocity that is so natural to all nations of African origin. These Islamites, whose chief glory it was dexterously to deprive their enemies of their heads, attach them to their saddle-bows, and afterward display them as trophies on the

---

Tres vezes si se burlava;
Que son malaas de creer
Las nuevas mui desseadas, etc.
Hollola en un jardin,
Entre mosquetta y jasmine, etc.

Viendose Moro con ella,
A penas los ojos alça;
Zelinda le asio la mano,
Un poco roxa y turbada;
Y al fin de infinitas guexas
Que en tales passos se passan,
Vistio se las ricas presas
Con las manos de su dama, etc.

battlements of their towers or at the entrance of their palaces; these restless and ungovernable warriors, who were ever ready to revolt against their rulers, to depose or to murder them, were the most tender, the most devoted, the most ardent of lovers. Their wives, though their domestic position was little superior to that of slaves, became, when they were beloved, the absolute sovereigns, the supreme divinities of those whose hearts they possessed. It was to please these idolized beings that the Moorish cavaliers sought distinction in the field; it was to shine in their eyes that they lavished their treasures and their lives—that they mutually endeavoured to eclipse each other in deeds of arms, in the splendour of their warlike exploits, and the Oriental magnificence of their fêtes.

It cannot now be determined whether the Moors derived this extraordinary union of softness and cruelty, of delicacy and barbarity—this generous rivalry in courage and in constancy from the Spaniards, or whether the Spaniards acquired these characteristics from the Moors. But when it is remembered that they do not belong to the Asiatic Arabs, from whom these gallant knights originally sprang; that they are found, even in a less degree, if possible, among these followers of Mohammed in that portion of Africa where their conquests have naturalized them; and, that after their departure from Spain, the Grenadians lost every trace of the peculiarly interesting and chivalrous qualities by which they had previously been so remarkably distinguished, there is some ground for the opinion that it was to the Spaniards that their Moslem neighbours were indebted for the existence of these national attributes. In truth, before the invasion of Spain by the Arabs, the courts of the Gothic kings had already offered knightly examples of a similar spirit. And after that event we find the cavaliers of Leon, Navarre, and Castile equally renowned for their achievements in war and their romantic devotion to the fair sex. The mere name of *the Cid* awakens in the mind recollections alike of tenderness and bravery. It should be remembered, too, that, long after the expulsion of the Moors from the Peninsula, the Spaniards maintained a reputation for gallantry far superior to that of the French, some portion of the spirit of which, though extinct among every other European nation, still lingers in Spain.

But, be this point decided as it may, it is not to be disputed that the daughters of Grenada merited the devotion which they inspired: they were perhaps the most fascinating women in the world. We find in the narrative of a Moorish historian, who wrote at Grenada during the reign of Mohammed the Old, the following description of his countrywomen:

"Their beauty is remarkable; but the loveliness which strikes the beholder at first sight afterward receives its principal charm from the grace and gentleness of their manners. In stature they are above the middle height, and of delicate and slender proportions. Their long black hair descends to the earth. Their teeth embellish with the whiteness of alabaster, vermillion lips, which perpetually smile with a bewitching air. The constant use which they make of the most exquisite perfumes, gives a freshness and brilliancy to their complexions possessed by no other Mohammedan women. Their walking, their dancing, their every movement, is distinguished by a graceful softness, an ease, a lightness, which surpasses all their other charms. Their conversation is lively and sensible, and their fine intellects are constantly displayed in brilliant wit or judicious sentiments."

The dress of these elegant females was composed, as that of the Turkish women still is, of a long tunic of linen confined by a cincture, of a *doliman* or Turkish dress with close sleeves, of wide trousers and Morocco slippers. The materials of their clothing were of the finest fabric, and were usually woven in stripes: they were embroidered with gold and silver, and profusely spangled with jewels. Their waving tresses floated over their shoulders; and a small cap, adorned with the richest gems, supported an embroidered veil, which fell nearly to the feet. The men were clothed in a similar manner: with them were carried in the girdle the purse, the handkerchief, and the poniard: a white, and sometimes a coloured, turban covered the head; and over the Turkish doliman they wore in summer a wide and flowing white robe, and in winter the *albornos* or African mantle. The only change made in their dress by the Moorish cavaliers when preparing for battle was the addition of a coat of mail, and an iron lining within their turbans.

It was the custom of the Grenadians to repair

every year, during the autumn, to the charming villas by which the city was surrounded. There they yielded themselves up to the pursuit of pleasure. The chase and the dance, music and feasting, occupied every hour.

The manners of those who participated in these national dances were in a high degree unreserved, as was the language of the songs and ballads in which they joined. Were it not for the contradictions in the human character, one might be surprised at this want of delicacy in a people who were capable of so much refinement of feeling. But, in general, nations of Oriental origin possess but little reserve in their manners: they have more of passion than sentiment, more of jealousy than delicacy in their haughty and excitable natures.

In giving these details, we have perhaps trespassed too long on the period of calm repose enjoyed by the kingdom of Grenada during the reign of Abouhadjad. That excellent sovereign, after having filled the throne for thirteen years, left his flourishing dominions to his son Joseph, who succeeded him without opposition, A.D. 1392, Heg. 795.

Joseph II. was desirous, in imitation of the

course pursued by his father, of maintaining the truce with the Christians. It was, however, soon disturbed by a fanatical hermit, who persuaded the Grand-master of Alcantara, Martin de Barbuda, a Portuguese, that he had been selected by Heaven as the chosen instrument for expelling the infidels from Spain. He promised the credulous Martin, in the name of God, that he should succeed in conquering the enemies of the Cross, and in carrying the city of Grenada by assault, without the loss of a single soldier. The infatuated grand-master, convinced of the certainty of the fulfilment of this promise, immediately sent ambassadors to Joseph, with orders to declare to that sovereign, in his name, that, since the religion of Mohammed was false and detestable, and that of Jesus Christ the only true and saving faith, he, Martin de Barbuda, defied the King of Grenada to a combat of two hundred Mussulmans against one hundred Christians, upon condition that the vanquished nation should instantly adopt the faith of the conquerors.

The reception these ambassadors met with may be easily imagined. Joseph could scarcely restrain the indignation of his people. The envoys, driven contemptuously away, returned to the presence of the grand-master, who, surprised at receiving no response to his proposal, soon assembled a thousand foot-soldiers and three hundred cavaliers, and hastened to the conquest of Grenada under the guidance of the prophetic hermit.

The King of Castile, Henry III., who desired to preserve peace with the followers of the Prophet at the commencement of a reign during which his own dominions were but ill at rest, was no sooner informed of the enterprise of Barbuda, than he sent him positive orders not to cross the frontiers; but that dignitary replying that he ought to obey the commands of Jehovah rather than those of any earthly master, proceeded on his way. The governors of the different cities through which he passed on his route endeavoured, though vainly, to arrest his progress; but the people overwhelmed him with homage, and everywhere added to the number of his forces.

The army of the grand-master amounted to six thousand men, when, in A.D. 1394, Heg. 798, he entered the country which his folly taught him to regard as already in his possession. In attacking the first castle at which he arrived, three soldiers were killed and their fanatical commander himself wounded. Surprised beyond measure at beholding his own blood flow and three soldiers fall, he summoned the anchorite into his presence, and sedately demanded what this meant, after his express promise that not a single champion of the true faith should perish. The fanatic replied, that the word he had pledged extended only to regular battles. Barbuda complained no more, and presently perceived the approach of a Moorish army composed of fifty thousand men. The conflict soon commenced: the grand-master and his three hundred mounted followers perished in the field, after having performed prodigies of valour. The remainder of the Spanish army were either taken prisoners or put to flight; and the silence of historians respecting the hermit, leads to the opinion that he was not among the last to seek safety at a distance from the scene of action.

This foolish enterprise did not interrupt the good understanding subsisting between the two nations. The King of Castile disavowed all approval of the conduct of Martin de Barbuda, and Joseph long continued to reign with honour and tranquillity. But he was at last poisoned, it is said, by a magnificent robe which he received from his secret enemy, the King of Fez, through the ambassadors of that sovereign. Historians assert that this garment was impregnated with a terrible poison, which caused the death of the unfortunate Joseph by the most horrible torments. The peculiar effects it produced was that of detaching the flesh from the bones, the misery of the wretched sufferer enduring for the protracted period of thirty days.

Mohammed IX., the second son of this hapless monarch, who, even during the lifetime of his father, had excited commotions in the realm, usurped the crown that of right belonged to his elder brother Joseph, whom he caused to be confined in prison.

Mohammed was courageous, and possessed some talents for war. Allied with the King of Tunis, who joined his fleet with that of Grenada, he broke the truce maintained with Castile during the two preceding reigns, and at first gained some advantages over his adversaries; but the Infant Don Ferdinand, the uncle and tutor of the young king John II., was not long in avenging the cause of Spain.

Mohammed IX. died in the year 1408, Heg

811. When the expiring monarch became conscious that his end was rapidly approaching, desirous of securing the crown to his son, he sent one of his principal officers to the prison of his brother Joseph, with orders to cut off the head of the royal occupant. The officer found Joseph engaged in a game of chess with an iman :* he sorrowfully announced the mournful commission with which he was charged. The prince, without manifesting any emotion at the communication, only demanded time to conclude his game; and the officer could not refuse this slight favour. While the philosophical Mussulman continued to play, a second messenger arrived, bearing the news of the death of the usurper, and of the proclamation of Joseph as his successor to the throne.

The people of Grenada were happy under the rule of the good King Joseph III. So far was he from avenging himself upon those who had aided his brother in depriving him of his rights, that he lavished favours and offices on them, and educated the son of Mohammed in the same manner as his own children. When his councillors blamed him for a degree of indulgence

* Mohammedan priest.

which they regarded as hazardous, "Allow me," replied the sovereign, "to deprive my enemies of all excuse for having preferred my younger brother to me!"

This excellent prince was often obliged to take arms against the Christians. He was so unfortunate as to lose some cities, but he preserved the respect and affection of his subjects, and died lamented by the whole kingdom, after a reign of fifteen years, A.D. 1423, Heg. 927.

After the death of Joseph the state was distracted by civil wars. Mohammed X. Abenazar, or the *Left-handed*, the son and successor of that benevolent king, was banished from the throne by Mohammed XI. *El Zugair*, or the Little, who preserved his ill-gotten power but two years. The Abencerrages, a powerful tribe* at Grenada, re-established Mohammed the Left-handed in his former place, and his competitor perished on the scaffold.

About four years after the death of Joseph, the Spaniards renewed their inroads into Grenada, and carried fire and sword to the very gates of the capital. All the neighbouring fields were devastated; the crops were burned and the vil-

* See Note H, page 225.

lages destroyed. John II., who then reigned in Castile, wishing to add to the miseries he had already occasioned these unhappy people the still greater misfortune of civil war, instigated the proclamation at Grenada of a certain Joseph Alhamar, a grandson of that Mohammed the Red so basely assassinated at Seville by Peter the Cruel.

All the discontented spirits in the kingdom joined the faction of Joseph Alhamar; and the Zegris, a powerful tribe, who were at enmity with the Abencerrages, lent their aid to the usurper. Mohammed Abenazar was again driven from the capital, A.D. 1432, Heg. 836, and Joseph IV. Alhamar possessed his dominions six months. At the termination of that time he expired.

Mohammed the Left-handed once more resumed his royal seat; but, after thirteen years of misfortune, this unhappy prince was again deposed for the third time, and imprisoned by one of his nephews, named Mohammed XII. the Osmin, who was himself afterward dethroned[*] by his own brother Ismael, and ended his days

[*] A.D. 1453, Heg. 857.

in the same dungeon in which his uncle Mohammed Abenazar had languished.

All these revolutions did not prevent the Christian and Moorish governors who commanded on their respective frontiers from making incessant irruptions into the enemy's country. Sometimes a little troop of cavalry or infantry surprised a village, massacred the inhabitants, pillaged their houses, and carried away their flocks. Sometimes an army suddenly appeared in a fertile plain, devastated the fields, uprooted the vines, felled the trees, besieged and took some town or fortress, and retired with their booty. This kind of warfare was ruinous, most of all, to the unfortunate cultivator of the soil. The Grenadian dominions suffered so much during the reign of Ismael II., that the king was compelled to cause immense forests to be cleared for the support of his capital, which then drew scarcely any supplies from the vast and fertile *vega* which had been so often desolated by the Spaniards.

Ismael II. left the crown to his son Mulei-Hassem, a young and highly courageous prince, who, profiting by the disastrous condition of Castile under the deplorable reign of Henry IV. the

Impotent, carried his arms into the centre of Andalusia. The success that marked the commencement of the reign of this sovereign, together with his talents and warlike ardour, tempted the Moors to believe that they might yet recover their former greatness. But the occurrence at this juncture of a great and unlooked-for event, arrested the victorious progress of Mulei-Hassam, and prepared the way for the total ruin of his kingdom.

Isabella of Castile, the sister of Henry the Impotent, notwithstanding the opposition of her brother and the intervention of almost insurmountable obstacles, espoused Ferdinand the Catholic, the king of Sicily, and heir presumptive of the kingdom of Aragon.* This marriage, by uniting the two most powerful monarchs of Spain, gave a fatal blow to the prosperity of the Moors, which they had been able to maintain, even in the degree in which it now existed, only through the divisions which had hitherto perpetually prevailed among their Christian opponents.

Either of the two enemies, now unitedly arrayed against them, had been singly sufficient

* A.D. 1469, Heg 874.

to overwhelm the Mussulmans. Ferdinand was alike politic, able, and adroit. He was pliant, and, at the same time, firm; cautious to a degree sometimes amounting to pusillanimity; cunning even to falsehood, and endowed in an extraordinary degree with the power of discerning at a single glance all the various means of attaining a particular end. Isabella was of a prouder and more noble nature; endowed with heroic courage and the most unyielding constancy of purpose, she was admirably qualified for the pursuit and accomplishment of any enterprise to which she might direct the energies of her powerful mind. The exalted endowments of one of these royal personages have been employed to ennoble the character of the other. Ferdinand often played the part of a weak, perfidious woman, negotiating only to deceive; whereas Isabella was always the high-souled sovereign, advancing openly to her purposes, and marching directly to honourable conflict and generous triumph.

No sooner had these distinguished individuals secured possession of their respective kingdoms, suppressed all domestic disturbances, and effected peaceful arrangements with foreign powers, than they mutually resolved to concentrate all their efforts for the annihilation of the Mohammedan dominion in Spain.

This century seemed destined to be marked by the glory of the Spaniards. In addition to the immense advantages afforded them by the union of their forces, Ferdinand and Isabella were surrounded by the wisest and most experienced advisers. The celebrated Cardinal Ximenes, at one time a simple monk, was now at the head of their councils; and that able minister "*led*," as he himself averred, "*all Spain by his girdle!*" The civil wars with which the Peninsula had been so long disturbed, had created among the Christian powers a host of brave soldiers and excellent commanders. Among the latter were particularly distinguished the Count de Cabra, the Marquis of Cadiz, and the famous Gonzalvo of Cordova, whose just claim to the surname of *the Great Captain*, given him by his countrymen, the lapse of time has only served to confirm. The public treasury, which had been exhausted by the lavish prodigality of Henry, was soon replenished by the rigid economy of Isabella, aided by a bull from the pope, permitting the royal appropriation of the ecclesiastical revenues. The troops were numerous and admirably disciplined, and the emulation which existed between the Castilians and Aragonians redoubled the valour of both. Everything, in short, prognosticated the downfall of the last remaining throne of the Moors.

Its royal champion, Mulei-Hassem, was not dismayed, however, even by such an accumulation of danger. He was the first to break the truce, by taking forcible possession of the city of Zahra, A.D. 1481, Heg. 886. Ferdinand despatched ambassadors to the Moslem court to complain of this breach of faith; with orders, at the same time, to demand the ancient tribute which had been paid by the kings of Grenada to the sovereigns of Castile.

"I know," replied Mulei-Hassem, when the envoys of the Spanish prince had delivered their message, "I know that some of my predecessors rendered you tribute in pieces of gold; but *this* is the only metal now coined in the national mint of Grenada!" And, as he spoke, the stern and haughty monarch presented the head of his lance to the Spanish ambassadors.

The army of Ferdinand first marched upon Alhamar, a very strong fortress in the neighbourhood of Grenada, and particularly famous for the magnificent baths with which it had been embellished by the Moorish kings. The place was taken by surprise, and thus a war was lighted up that was destined to be extinguished only with the last expiring sigh of Grenada.

Victory seemed at first to be equally poised between the two contending powers. The King of Grenada possessed ample resources in troops, artillery, and treasure. He might have long maintained the contest, but for an act of imprudence which precipitated him into an abyss of misfortune from which he was never afterward able to extricate himself.

The wife of Mulei-Hassem, named Aixa, belonged, before her marriage with the king, to one of the most important of the Grenadian tribes. The offspring of this marriage was a son named Boabdil, whose right it was to succeed to his father's throne. But the reckless Mulei repudiated his wife at the instance of a Christian slave, of whom he became enamoured, and who governed the doting monarch at will. This act of cruelty and injustice was the signal for civil war. The injured Aixa, in concert with her son, excited her relatives and friends,

P

and a large number of the inhabitants of the capital, to throw off their allegiance to their sovereign.

Mulei-Hassem was eventually driven from the city, and Boabdil assumed the title of king. Thus father and son were involved in a contest for the possession of a crown, of which Ferdinand was seeking to deprive them both.

To add to the misfortunes which were already fast crushing this distracted and miserable country beneath their weight, another aspirant to the throne presented himself, in the person of a brother of Mulei-Hassem named Zagel. This prince, at the head of a band of Moorish adventurers, had succeeded in obtaining some important advantages over the Spaniards in the defiles of Malaga, A.D. 1483, Heg. 888.

His achievements having won for him the hearts of his countrymen, Zagel now conceived the design of dethroning his brother and nephew, and of appropriating the dominions of both to himself. Thus a third faction arose to increase the dissensions of the state.

Boabdil still held insecure possession of the capital; and, desirous of attempting some action, the brilliancy of which would reanimate the hopes and confidence of a party that was ready to abandon him, he sallied forth at the head of a small force, with the intention of surprising Lucena, a city belonging to the Castilians.

But the ill-fated Boabdil was made a prisoner in this expedition.

He was the first Moorish king who had ever been a captive to the Spaniards. Ferdinand lavished on him the attentions due to misfortune, and caused him to be conducted to Cordova, attended by an escort.

The old king, Mulei-Hassem, seized this opportunity to repossess himself of the crown of which his rebellious son had deprived him, and, in spite of the party of Zagel, he again became master of his capital. But the restored monarch could oppose but a feeble resistance to the progress of the Spaniards, who were rapidly reducing his cities and advancing nearer to his devoted capital. Within the walls of that city the wretched inhabitants were madly warring against one another, as if unconscious of the destruction that was fast approaching them from without. To increase the sanguinary feuds which already so surely presaged their destruction, the Catholic sovereigns had become the al lies of the captive Boabdil, engaging to assist him in his efforts against his father on condition that he should pay them a tribute of twelve thousand crowns of gold, acknowledge himself their vassal, and deliver certain strong places into their hands. The base Boabdil acceded to everything; and, aided by the politic Spanish princes, hastened again to take arms against his father.

The kingdom of Grenada was now converted into one wide field of carnage, where Mulei-Hassem, Boabdil, and Zagel were furiously contending for the mournful relics of their country.

The Spaniards, in the mean time, marched rapidly from one conquest to another, sometimes under pretext of sustaining their ally Boabdil, and often in open defiance of the treaty they had formed with that prince; but always carefully feeding the fire of discord, while they were despoiling each of the three rival parties, and leaving to the vanquished inhabitants their laws, their customs, and the free exercise of their religion

In the midst of these frightful scenes of calamity and crime, old Mulei-Hassem died, either worn out by grief and misfortune, or through the agency of his ambitious brother. This event occurred A.D. 1485, Heg. 890.

Ferdinand had now rendered himself master of all the western part of the kingdom of Grenada, and Boabdil agreed to divide with Zagel the remnant of this desolated state. The city of Grenada was retained by Boabdil, while Gaudix and Almeria fell to the share of Zagel. The war was not the less vigorously prosecuted in consequence of this arrangement; and the unprincipled Zagel, doubting his ability long to retain the cities in his possession, sold them to King Ferdinand in consideration of an annual pension.

By virtue of this treaty, the Catholic sovereigns took possession of the purchased cities; and the traitor Zagel even lent the aid of his arms to the Christian army, the more speedily to overthrow the royal power of his nephew, and thereby terminate the existence of his expiring country.

All that now remained to the Mussulmans was the single city of Grenada. There Boabdil still reigned; and, exasperated by misfortune, he vented his rage and despair in acts of barbarous cruelty towards its wretched inhabitants.

Ferdinand and Isabella, disregarding the conditions of their pretended alliance with this now powerless prince, summoned him to surrender his capital, in compliance, as they said, with the terms of a secret treaty, which they affirmed had been concluded between them. Boabdil protested against this perfidious conduct. But there was no time allowed for complaint: he must successfully defend himself, or cease to reign. The Moorish prince adopted, therefore, to say the least, the most heroic alternative; and resolved to defend to the last what remained to him of his once beautiful and flourishing country.

The Spanish sovereign, at the head of an army of sixty thousand men, the flower and chivalry of the united kingdoms of Castile and Aragon, laid siege to Grenada on the 9th of May, 1491, and in the 897th year of the Hegira.

This great city, as has been already mentioned, was defended by strong ramparts, flanked by a multitude of towers, and by numerous other fortifications, built one above the other. Notwithstanding the civil wars which had inundated it with blood, Grenada still enclosed within its walls more than two hundred thousand inhabitants. Every brave Moorish cavalier who still remained true to his country, its religion, and its laws, had here taken refuge. Despair redoubled their strength in this last desperate struggle; and had these fierce and intrepid warriors been guided by a more worthy chief than Boabdil, their noble constancy might still have saved them; but this weak and ferocious monarch hesitated not, on the slightest suspicion, to consign his most faithful defenders to the axe of the executioner. Thus he became daily more and more an object of hatred and contempt to the Grenadians, by whom he was surnamed *Zogoybi*, that is to say, *the Little King*. The different tribes now grew dissatisfied and dispirited, especially the numerous and powerful tribe of the Abencerrages. The alfaquis and the imans, also, loudly predicted the approaching downfall of the Moorish empire; and nothing upheld the sinking courage of the people against the pressure of a foreign foe and the tyranny of their own rulers but their unconquerable horror of the Spanish yoke.

The Catholic soldiers, on the other hand, elated by their past success, regarded themselves as invincible, and never for a moment doubted the certainty of their triumph. They were commanded, also, by leaders to whom they were devotedly attached : Ponce de Leon, marquis of Cadiz, Henry de Guzman, duke of Medina, Mendoza, Aguillar, Villena, and Gonzalvo of Cordova, together with many other famous captains, accompanied their victorious king. Isabella, too, whose virtues excited the highest respect, and whose affability and grace won for her the affectionate regard of all, had repaired to the camp of her husband with the Infant and the Infantas, and attended by the most brilliant court in Europe. This politic princess, though naturally grave and serious, wisely accommodated herself to the existing circumstances. She mingled fêtes and amusements with warlike toil: jousts and tournaments delighted at intervals the war-worn soldiery; and dances, games, and illuminations filled up the delicious summer evenings.

Queen Isabella was the animating genius that directed everything; a gracious word from her was a sufficient recompense for the most gallant achievement; and her look alone had power to transform the meanest soldier into a hero.

Abundance reigned in the Christian camp;

while joy and hope animated every heart. But within the beleaguered city, mutual distrust, universal consternation, and the prospect of inevitable destruction, had damped the courage and almost annihilated the hopes of the wretched inhabitants.

The siege, nevertheless, lasted for nine months. The cautious commander of the Christian army did not attempt to carry by assault a place so admirably fortified. After having laid waste the environs, therefore, he waited patiently until famine should deliver the city into his hands. Satisfied with battering the ramparts and repelling the frequent sorties of the Moors, he never engaged in any decisive action, but daily hemmed in more closely the chafed lion that could not now escape his toils.

Accident one night set fire to the pavilion of Isabella, and the spreading conflagration consumed every tent in the camp. But Boabdil derived no advantage from this disaster. The queen directed that a city should supply the place of the ruined camp, to convince the enemies of the cross that the siege would never be raised until Grenada should come into possession of the conquering Spaniards. This great and extraordinary design, so worthy the genius of Isabella, was executed in eighty days. The Christian camp thus became a walled city; and Santa Fé still exists as a monument of the piety and perseverance of the heroic Queen of Castile.

At last, oppressed by famine, less frequently successful than at first in the partial engagements that were constantly taking place under the walls, and abandoned by Africa, from which there were no attempts made to relieve them, the Moors now felt the necessity of a surrender.

Gonzalvo of Cordova was empowered by the conquerors to arrange the articles of capitulation. These provided that the people of Grenada should recognise Ferdinand and Isabella, and their royal successors, as their rightful sovereigns; that all their Christian captives should be released without ransom; that the Moors should continue to be governed by their own laws; should retain their national customs, their judges, half the number of their mosques, and the free exercise of their faith; that they should be permitted either to keep or sell their property, and to retire to Africa, or to any other country they might choose, while, at the same time, they should not be compelled to leave their native land. It was also agreed that Boabdil should have assigned to him a rich and ample domain in the Alpuxares, of which he should possess the entire command.

Such were the terms of capitulation, and but ill were they observed by the Spaniards. Boabdil fulfilled his part of the stipulations some days before the time specified, in consequence of being informed that his people, roused by the representations of the imans, wished to break off the negotiations, and to bury themselves beneath the ruins of the city rather than suffer their desolate and deserted homes to be profaned by the intruding foot of the spoiler.

The wretched Moslem prince hastened therefore to deliver the keys of the city, and of the fortresses of the Albazin and the Alhambra, into the hands of Ferdinand.

Entering no more, after this mournful ceremony, within the walls where he no longer retained any authority, Boabdil took his melancholy journey, accompanied by his family and a small number of followers, to the petty dominions which were now all that remained to him of the once powerful and extensive empire of his ancestors.

When the cavalcade reached an eminence from which the towers of Grenada might still be discerned, the wretched exile turned his last sad regards upon the distant city, amid ill-suppressed tears and groans. *"You do well,"* said Aixa, his mother, *"to weep like a woman for the throne you could not defend like a man!"*

But the now powerless Boabdil could not long endure existence as a subject in a country where he had reigned as a sovereign: he crossed the Mediterranean to Africa, and there he ended his days on the battle-field.

Ferdinand and Isabella made their public entrance into Grenada on the 1st of January, 1492, through double ranks of soldiers, and amid the thunder of artillery. The city seemed deserted; the inhabitants fled from the presence of the conquerors, and concealed their tears and their despair within the innermost recesses of their habitations.

The royal victors repaired first to the grand mosque, which was consecrated as a Christian church, and where they rendered thanks to God for the brilliant success that had crowned their arms. While the sovereigns fulfilled this pious duty, the Count de Tendilla, the new governor of Grenada, elevated the triumphant cross, and the standards of Castile and St. James, on the highest towers of the Alhambra.

Thus fell this famous city, and thus perished the power of the Moors of Spain, after an existence of seven hundred and eighty-two years from the first conquest of the country by Tarik.

It may now be proper briefly to remark upon the principal causes of the extinction of the national independence of the kingdom of Grenada.

The first of these arose from the peculiar character of the Moors: from that spirit of inconstancy, that love of novelty, and that unceasing inquietude, which prompted them to such frequent change of their rulers; which multiplied factions among them, and constantly convulsed the empire with internal discords, expending its strength and power in dissensions at home, and thus leaving it defenceless against foreign enemies. The Moors may also be reproached with an extravagant fondness for architectural magnificence, splendid fêtes, and other expensive entertainments, which aided in exhausting the national treasury at times when protracted warfare scarcely ever permitted this most fertile region of the earth to reproduce the crops the Spaniards had destroyed. But, more than all, they were a people without an established code of laws, that only permanent basis of the prosperity of nations. And then, too, a despotic form of government, which deprives men of patriotism, induced each individual to regard his virtues and attainments merely as affording the means of personal consideration, and not, as they should be considered, the property of his country.

These grave defects in the national character of the Moors were redeemed by many excellent qualities, which even the Spaniards admitted them to possess. In battle they were no less brave and prudent than their Christian antagonists, though inferior in skill and discipline. They excelled them, however, in the art of attack. Adversity never long overwhelmed them; they saw in misfortune the will of Heaven, and without a murmur submitted to it. Their favourite dogma of fatalism doubtless contributed to this result. Fervently devoted to the laws of Mohammed, they obeyed with great exactness his humane injunctions respecting almsgiving:* they bestowed on the poor not only food and

* See Note I, page 226.

money, but a portion of their grain, fruit, and flocks, and of every kind of merchandise. In the towns and throughout the country, the indigent sick were collected, attended, and nursed with the most assiduous care. Hospitality, so sacred from the remotest time among the Arabs, was not less carefully observed among the people of Grenada, who seemed to take peculiar pleasure in its exercise. The following touching anecdote is told in illustration of the powerful influence of this principle. A stranger, bathed in blood, sought refuge from the officers of justice under the roof of an aged Moor. The old man concealed him in his house. But he had scarcely done so before a guard arrived to demand possession of the murderer, and, at the same time, to deliver to the horror-stricken Mussulman the dead body of his son, whom the stranger had just assassinated. Still the aged father would not give up his guest. When the guard, however, were gone, he entreated the assassin to leave him. "*Depart from me,*" he cried, "*that I may be at liberty to pursue thee!*"

These Moslems were but little known to the historians by whom they have been so often calumniated. Polished, enthusiastic, hospitable, brave, and chivalrous, but haughty, passionate, inconstant, and vindictive, their unfortunate fate entitles them, at least, to compassion and sympathy, while their virtues may well excite respect and interest.

After their final defeat, many of the followers of the Prophet retired to Africa. Those who remained in Grenada suffered greatly from the persecution and oppression to which they were subjected by their new masters. The article in their last treaty with the Spaniards, which formally ensured their religious freedom, was grossly violated by the Catholics, who compelled the Mussulmans to abjure their national faith by force, terror, and every other unworthy means.

At last, outraged beyond endurance by this want of good faith, and wrought to desperation by the cruelties they were compelled to endure, in the year 1500 the Moors attempted to revolt against their oppressors. Their efforts were, however, unavailing: Ferdinand marched in person against them, repressed by force of arms the struggles of a people whom he designated as rebels, and, sword in hand, administered the rite of baptism to more than fifty thousand captive Moslems.

The successors of Ferdinand, Charles V. and especially Philip II., continued to harass the Moors.* The Inquisition was established in the city of Grenada, and all the terrors of that dreaded institution were added to gentler means for the conversion of the infidels to Christianity. Their children were taken from them to be educated in accordance with the precepts of that religion whose Adorable Founder enjoined peace, mercy, and forbearance upon his followers, and forbade the practice of injustice and cruelty in every form.

Yielding to the promptings of despair, this crushed and wretched remnant of a once powerful and glorious nation again flew to arms in the year 1569, and executed the most terrible vengeance upon the Catholic priesthood. Mohammed-ben-Ommah, the new king whom they chose to direct their destinies, and who was

* The edicts of Charles V., which were renewed and rendered more severe by Philip II., directed an entire change in the peculiar domestic habits and manners of the Moors, prescribed their adoption of the Spanish costume and language, forbade their women to wear veils, interdicted the use of the bath and the celebration of their national dances, and ordered that all their children from the age of five to fifteen should be registered, that they might be sent to Catholic schools.

Q

said to have sprung from the cherished race of the Ommiades, several times gave battle to his opponents in the mountains of the Alpuxares, where he sustained the cause of his injured countrymen for the space of two years. At the end of that time he was assassinated by his own people. His successor shared the same fate, and the Mussulmans were again compelled to submit to a yoke their revolt had rendered even more intolerable than before.

Finally, King Philip III. totally banished the Moors from Spain. The depopulation thus produced inflicted a wound upon that kingdom, from the effects of which it has never since recovered.

More than one hundred and fifty thousand of this persecuted race took refuge in France, where Henry IV. received them with great humanity. A small number also concealed themselves in the recesses of the Alpuxares; but the greatest part of the expatriated Islamites sought a home in Africa. There their descendants still drag out a miserable existence under the despotic rule of the sovereigns of Morocco, and unceasingly pray that they may be restored to their beloved Grenada.

NOTES.

FIRST EPOCH.

A, page 25.

Until they embrace Islamism, &c

The word *Islamism* is derived from *islam*, which signifies *consecration to God.*

The brief synopsis given in the text of the principles of the Mohammedan religion, is literally rendered by the author from several different chapters of the Koran. These precepts are there to be found almost lost amid a mass of absurdities, repetitions, and incoherent rhapsodies. Yet, throughout the entire work, there are occasionally bright gleams of fervid eloquence or pure morality. Mohammed never speaks on his own authority; he pretends always to be prompted by the angel Gabriel, who repeats to him the commands of the Most High: the Prophet does but listen and repeat them. The angelic messenger has taken care to enter into a multitude of details, not only in relation to religion, but also to legislation and government. And thus it happens that the Koran is regarded by the Mussulmans as their standard, no less for c'vil than for moral law. One half of this book is written in verse, and the remainder in poetical prose. Mohammed possessed great poetical talent; an endowment so highly esteemed by his countrymen. that they were in the habit of assembling at **Mecca** to pronounce judgment on the different poems affixed by their respective authors to the walls of the temple of the Caaba; and the individual in whose favour the popular voice decided was crowned with great solemnity. When the second chapter of the Koran, *Labia ebn rabia*, appeared on the walls, the most famous poet of the time, who had previously posted up a rival production of his own, tore it down, and acknowledged himself conquered by the Prophet.

Mohammed was not altogether the monster of cruelty so many authors represent him to have been. He often displayed much humanity towards offenders who were in his power, and even forgave personal injuries. One of the most unrelenting of his enemies, named Caab, on whose head a price had been set, had the audacity suddenly to appear in the mosque at Medina while Mohammed was preaching to the multitude. Caab recited some verses which he had composed in honour of the Prophet. Mohammed listened to them with pleasure, embraced the poet, and invested him with his own mantle. This precious garment was afterward bought by one of the caliphs of the East, from the family of Caab, for the sum of twenty thousand drachms, and became the pride of those Asiatic sovereigns, who wore it only on the occasion of some solemn festival.

The last moments of Mohammed would seem to prove that he was far from possessing an ignoble mind. Feeling his end approaching, he repaired to the mosque, supported by his friend Ali. Mounting the tribune, he made a prayer, and then, turning to the assembly, uttered these words: "Mussulmans, I am about to die. No one, therefore, need any longer fear me ; if I have struck any one among you, here is my breast, let him strike me in return : if I have wrongfully taken the property of any one, here is my purse, let him remunerate himself : if I have humbled any one, let him now spurn me: I surrender myself to the justice of my countrymen!" The people sobbed aloud: one individual alone demanded three drachms of the dying Prophet, who instantly discharged the debt with interest. After this he took an affectionate leave of the brave Medinians who had so faithfully defended him, gave liberty to his slaves, and ordered the arrangements for his funeral. His last interview with his wife and daughter, and Omar and Ali, his friends and disciples, was marked by much tenderness. Sorrow and lamentation were universal throughout Arabia on this occasion; and his daughter Fatima died of grief for his loss.

The respect and veneration entertained by his followers for Mohammed is almost inconceivable. Their doctors have gravely asserted in their writings that the world was created for him; that the first thing made was light, and that that light became the substance of the soul of Mohammed, etc. Some of them have maintained that the Alcoran was uncreated, while others have adopted a contrary opinion; and out of these discordant views have arisen numerous sects, and even wars that have deluged Asia with blood.

The life of Mohammed was terminated by poison, which had been administered to him some years before by a Jewess named Zainab, whose brother had been slain by Ali. This woman, to avenge the death of her brother, poisoned some roasted lamb which she served up for the Prophet. Scarcely had he put a morsel of it into his mouth, when, instantly rejecting it, he exclaimed that the meat was poisoned. Notwithstanding the prompt use of antidotes, the injurious consequences were so severe, that he suffered from them during the remainder of his life, and died four years after, in the sixty-third year of his age.

B, page 27.
Kaled, surnamed the Sword of God, &c.

The feats of arms ascribed by historians to Kaled resemble those of a hero of romance. He was at first the enemy of the great Arabian leader, and vanquished that commander in the conflict of *Aheh*, the only battle which Mohammed ever lost. Having afterward become a zealous Mussulman, he subjugated such parts of the Mohammedan dominions as had revolted after the death of the Prophet, opposed the armies of Heraclius, conquered Syria, Palestine, and a part of Persia, and came off victor in numerous single combats in which he was at different times engaged: always challenging to an encounter of this kind the general of the hostile army. The following anecdote will illustrate his character. Kaled besieged the city of Bostra. The Greek governor, named Romain, under pretence of making a sortie, passed the walls with his troops, and arranged them in order of battle in front of the Mussulman army. At the moment when he should have given the signal for the onset, the valiant Greek demanded an interview with Kaled. The two commanders, therefore, advanced into the centre of the space which separated the opposing armies. Romain declared to the Saracen general that he had determined not only to deliver the city to him, but to embrace the religion of the crescent: he at the same time expressed a fear that his soldiers, among whom he was by no means popular, intended to take his life, and intreated Kaled to protect him against their vengeance.

"The best thing you can do," replied the Moslem leader, "is immediately to accept a challenge to a single combat with me. Such an exhibition of courage will gain for you the respect of your troops, and we can treat together afterward!"

At these words, without waiting for a reply from the governor, the champion of Islamism drew his cimeter and attacked the unfortunate Romain, who defended himself with a trembling hand. At each blow inflicted by the redoubtable follower of the Prophet, Romain cried out, " Do you then wish to kill me?" "No," replied the Mussulman; "my only object is, to load you with honour; the more you are beaten, the more esteem you will acquire!" At last, when he had nearly deprived the poor Greek of life, Kaled gave up the contest, and shortly after took possession of the city: when he next saw the pusillanimous governor, he politely inquired after his health.

C, page 30.
The warlike tribes of the Bereberes, &c.

The name of the portion of Africa called *Barbary* is derived from the Bereberes. This people regarded themselves, with much appearance of truth, as the descendants of those Arabs who originally came into the country with Malek Yarfric, and who are often confounded with the ancient Numidians. Their language, which differs from that of every other people, is, in the opinion of some authors, a corruption of the Punic or Carthaginian. Divided into tribes and wandering among the mountains, this peculiar race still exists in the kingdom of Morocco. The Bereberes were never allied with the Moors, for whom they always entertained a feeling of enmity. Though at present under the dominion of the kings of Morocco as their religious head, they brave his displeasure and authority at will. They are formidable in consequence of their numbers, courage, and indomitable spirit of independence; and still preserve unimpaired the peculiar simplicity of their ancient manners and habits.

D, page 34.

Tarik, one of the most renowned captains of his time, &c.

Tarik landed at the foot of the Calpe Mountain, and took the city of Herculia, to which the Arabs gave the name of *Djebel Tarik*, of which we have made *Gibraltar*.

E, page 38.

During the remainder of the Caliphate of Yezid II., &c.

This caliph, the ninth of the Ommiades, ended his existence in a manner that at least merits pity. He was amusing himself one day with throwing grapes at his favourite female slave, who caught them in her mouth. This fruit, it must be remembered, is much larger in Syria than in Europe. Unfortunately, one of the grapes passed into the throat of the slave and instantly suffocated her. The despairing Yezid would not permit the interment of this dearest object of his affections, and watched incessantly beside the corpse for eight successive days. Being compelled at last, by the condition of the body, to separate himself from it, he died of grief, entreating, as he expired, that his remains might be interred in the same tomb with his beloved Hubabah.

SECOND EPOCH.

A, page 46.

He was soon after assassinated, &c.

Three Karagites (a name applied to a pre-eminently fanatical sect of Mussulmans), beholding the disorders created in the Arabian empire by the contentions of Ali, Moavias, and

Amrou, believed that they should perform a service that would be acceptable to God, and restore peace to their country, by simultaneously assassinating the three rivals. One of them repaired to Damascus, and wounded the usurper Moavias in the back; but the wound did not prove mortal. The confederate charged with the murder of Amrou, stabbed, by mistake, one of the friends of that rebel. The third, who had undertaken to despatch Ali, struck him as he was about to enter the mosque, and the virtuous caliph was the only one who fell a victim to the design of the assassins.

B, page 48.
Mervan II., the last caliph of the race, &c.

This Ommiade was surnamed *Alhemar,* that is to say, *The Ass :* an appellation which, in the East, is considered highly honourable, from the singular regard there entertained for that patient and indefatigable animal. Ariosto derived his touching episode of Isabella of Gallicia from the history of this prince. Mervan, being at one time in Egypt, became enamoured of a religious recluse whom he chanced to see there, and endeavoured to persuade her to break her monastic vows. Effectually to relieve herself from his persecutions, the young devotee promised him an ointment which would render him invulnerable, and volunteered to prove its efficacy on her own person. After having anointed her neck with the mixture, she requested the caliph to test the keenness of his cimeter on it, which the barbarian did ; and the result may be easily imagined.

C, page 48.
The names of Haroun al Raschid, &c.

Haroun al Raschid (which signifies Haroun the Just) was

greatly renowned in the East. He undoubtedly, in part, owed
his fame, as well as his surname, to the protection he afforded
to men of letters. His military exploits and his love of science prove this caliph to have been no ordinary man; but
then the glory of his achievements was tarnished by his cruelty to the Bermacides. These were a distinguished tribe
or family, descended from the ancient kings of Persia. They
had rendered the most signal services to the successive caliphs, and won the respect and affection of the whole empire.
Giaffar Barmacide, who was considered the most virtuous of
Mussulmans and the most eminent author of the age, was
the vizier of Haroun. He entertained a passionate regard for
Abassa, the beautiful and accomplished sister of the caliph,
and the princess reciprocated his affection; but the sovereign
made the most unreasonable opposition to the celebration
of their nuptials. This they effected, however, without his
knowledge; and for some time Haroun remained ignorant
of the union of the lovers. But, at the end of some years,
the caliph made a pilgrimage to Mecca, to which city, the
more effectually to secure the inviolability of his secret, the
Bermacide had sent his infant son to be reared. There the
representative of the Prophet, through the instrumentality of
a perfidious slave, became acquainted with all the circumstances of the deception that had been practised on him. It
would be difficult to believe the account of what followed,
but that the facts were so well authenticated throughout Asia.
Haroun caused his sister to be thrown into a well, commanded
that Giaffar should lose his head, and ordered every relative
of the unfortunate Bermacide to be put to death. The father
of the vizier, a venerable old man, respected throughout the
empire, which he had long governed, met his fate with the
most heroic firmness. Before he expired, he wrote these

words to the sanguinary despot: "*The accused departs first; the accuser will shortly follow. Both will appear in the presence of a Judge whom no arguments can deceive!*"

The implacable Haroun carried his vengeance so far as to forbid that any one should mention the names of his hapless victims. One of his subjects, named Mundir, had the courage to brave this edict, and publicly to pronounce the eulogy of the beloved Bermacides.

The tyrant commanded that the offending Mussulman should appear before him, and threatened him with punishment for what he had done.

"You can silence me only by inflicting death upon me!" replied Mundir: "that you have the power of doing; but you cannot extinguish the gratitude entertained by the whole empire for those virtuous ministers: even the ruins you have made of the monuments which they erected, speak of their fame in spite of you!" It is said that the monarch was touched by the words of this fearless defender of the dead, and that he commanded a golden plate to be presented to him.

Such was the famous caliph who bore the name of *the Just*. Almamon, his son, received no surname; but he deserved to be ranked with the wisest and the most virtuous of men. Some idea of his character may be formed from the following anecdote. It is recorded of him, that his viziers urged him to punish with death one of his relations who had taken arms against him, and caused himself to be proclaimed caliph. Almamon, however, rejected this sanguinary counsel, saying at the same time, "Alas! if they who have injured me, knew how much pleasure I experience in forgiving my enemies, they would hasten to appear before me to confess their faults!" This excellent prince was the munificent patron of science and the arts, and his reign formed the most brilliant epoch of the glorious days of the Arabs.

D, page 54.
Wars with the kings of Leon, and incursions into Catalonia, &c.

Historians do not agree concerning the precise period when Charlemagne entered Spain. It would appear, however, that it was during the reign of Abderamus that the emperor crossed the Pyrenees, took Pampeluna and Saragossa, and was attacked, during his retreat, in the defiles of Roncevaux, a place rendered famous in romantic literature by the death of Roland.

E, page 59.
A government that properly respected the rights of the people, &c.

The ancient laws of Aragon, known under the name of *Fore de Sobarbe*, limited the power of the sovereign by creating a balance for it in that of the *ricos Hombres*, and of a magistrate who bore the name of *Justice*.

F, page 60.
The celebrated school, &c.

The musical school, founded at Cordova by Ali-Zeriab, produced the famous Moussali, who was regarded by the Orientals as the greatest musician of his time. The music of the Moors did not consist, like ours, in the concord of different instruments, but simply in soft and tender airs, which the musicians sung to the accompaniment of the lute. Sometimes several voices and lutes executed the same air in unison. This simple style of music satisfied a people who were such passionate lovers of poetry, that their first desire, when listening to a singer, was to hear the words he uttered.

Moussali, who was the pupil of Ali-Zeriab at Cordova, became afterward, in consequence of his musical talents, the favourite of Haroun al Raschid, the celebrated caliph of the East. It is related that this prince, in consequence of a misunderstanding with one of his favourite wives, fell into such a state of melancholy that fears were entertained for his life Giaffar, the Bermacide, at that time the principal vizier of the caliph, entreated the poet Abbas-ben-Ahnaf to compose some verses on the subject of this quarrel. He did so, and they were sung in the presence of the prince by Moussali; and the royal lover was so softened by the sentiments of the poet and the melody of the musician, that he immediately flew to the feet of his fair enslaver, and a reconciliation took place between the disconsolate monarch and the offended beauty. The grateful slave sent twenty thousand drachms of gold to the poet and Moussali, and Haroun added forty thousand more to her gift.

G, page 66.
The statue of the beautiful Zahra, &c.

Mohammed, to discourage idolatry, forbade his followers, in the Koran, to make images in any form; but this injunction was very imperfectly observed. The Oriental caliphs adopted the custom of stamping their coins with an impression of their own features, as is proved by specimens still existing in the collections of the curious. On one side of these was represented the head of the reigning caliph, and on the other appeared his name, with some passages from the Alcoran. In the palaces of Bagdad, Cordova and Grenada, figures of animals, and sculpture of various kinds, both in gold and marble, abounded.

H, page 69.

The richest and most powerful, &c.

Some conception of the opulence of the caliphs of the West, during the palmy days of their prosperity, may be formed from the value of the gifts presented to Abderamus III. by one of his subjects, Abdoumalek-ben-Chien, on the occasion of his being appointed to the dignity of chief vizier. The articles composing this present are thus enumerated: Four hundred pounds of virgin gold; four hundred and twenty thousand sequins, in the form of ingots of silver; four hundred and twenty pounds of the wood of aloes; five hundred ounces of ambergris; three hundred ounces of camphor; thirty pieces of silk and cloth of gold; ten robes of the sable fur of Korassan; one hundred others, of less valuable fur; forty-eight flowing housings for steeds, a thousand bucklers; a hundred thousand arrows; gold tissues, from Bagdad; four thousand pounds of silk; thirty Persian carpets; eight hundred suits of armour for war horses; fifteen Arabian coursers for the caliph; a hundred for the use of his officers; twenty mules, saddled and caparisoned; forty youths and twenty young maidens, of rare beauty.

I, page 81.

About this time occurred the famous adventure of the seven sons of Lara, so celebrated in Spanish history and romance, and of which, as in some degree connected with Moorish history, we may briefly narrate the particulars.

These young warriors were brothers, the sons of Gonzalvo Gustos, a near relative of the first counts of Castile, and lords of Salas de Lara. Ruy Velasquez, brother-in-law of Gonzalvo Gustos, instigated by his wife, who pretended to have some cause of offence against the youngest of the seven brothers, meditated the execution of a horrible scheme for their destruction. He commenced by sending their father Gonzalvo on an embassy to the court of Cordova, making him, at the same time, the bearer of letters, in which he prayed the caliph to put the envoy to death, as the enemy of the crescent and its followers. The Mussulman sovereign, being unwilling to commit so barbarous an act, contented himself with retaining Gonzalvo as a prisoner. In the mean time, the perfidious Velasquez, under pretence of conducting an attack against the Moors, led his nephews into the midst of an ambuscade, where, overpowered by numbers, they all perished, after a most heroic defence, accompanied by circumstances which render their end truly affecting. The barbarous uncle sent the gory heads of the murdered youths to the royal palace of Cordova, and caused them to be presented to the unhappy father, in a golden dish covered with a veil. No sooner did Gonzalvo behold the ghastly contents of the dish, than he fell to the earth, deprived of sense. The Caliph of the West, filled with indignation at the demoniac cruelty of Velasquez, restored his captive to liberty. But the foe of his race was too powerful to permit the childless Gonzalvo to avenge the murder of his offspring. He attempted, indeed, to do so; but old age had deprived him of his former strength and vigour. With his wife, therefore, he mourned in solitude over the untimely fate of his sons, and entreated Heaven to permit him to follow them to the tomb: but a champion of his cause unexpectedly arose in the person of an illegitimate son of Gonzalvo's at the Moorish court. When this boy had attained the age of twelve years, he was informed of his parentage by his mother, who was the sister of the sovereign of Cordova, and of the wrongs which his father had suffered.

The heroic youth, who bore the name of *Mendarra Gonzalvo*, resolved to become the avenger of his brothers. Hastening to execute his purpose, he left Cordova, challenged Valasquez, and slew him. Cutting off the head of his father's foe, he sought with his burden the presence of the old man, demanded to be acknowledged as his son, and admitted into the Christian church. The wife of Gonzalvo joyfully consented to receive the brave Mendarra as her son, and he was solemnly adopted by the venerable pair. The wife of Velasquez, who, it will be remembered, had instigated the ferocious uncle to his murderous deed, was stoned to death and afterward burned. It is from this valiant Mendarra Gonzalvo that the Mauriques de Lara, one of the most important Spanish families, seek to trace their descent.

THIRD EPOCH.

A, page 86.

Three bishops of Catalonia, &c.

These three bishops of Catalonia, who died fighting for the Mussulmans at the battle of Albakara, which took place in the year 1010, were Arnaulpha, bishop of Vic ; Accia, bishop of Barcelona; and Othon, bishop of Girona.

B, page 91.

And equally ready, when enjoying the favour of the sovereign, to displease him, if it should be necessary to do so, &c.

Rodrigue Dias de Bivar, surnamed *the Cid*, so well known by his affection for Chimena and his duel with the Count Gormas, has been the subject of many poems, novels, and romances in the Spanish tongue. Without crediting all the extraordinary adventures ascribed to this hero by his countrymen, it is proved by the testimony of reputable historians, that the Cid was not only the bravest and most dreaded warrior of his time, but one of the most virtuous and generous of men. De Bivar was already famed for his exploits while Castile was still under the dominion of Ferdinand I. When the successor of that monarch, Sancho II., endeavoured to despoil his sister Uraque of the city of Zamora, this champion of the oppressed, with noble firmness, represented to the king that he was about being guilty of an act of injustice, by which he would violate, at the same time, the laws of honour and the ties of blood. The offended Sancho exiled the Cid, but was soon after obliged by necessity to recall him. When the treacherous assassination of Sancho, while encamped before Zamora, entitled his brother Alphonso to the throne, the Castilians were anxious that their new sovereign should disavow, by a solemn oath, having had any agency in the murder of his brother. No one dared demand of the king to take this oath except the Cid, who constrained him to pronounce it aloud at the same altar where his coronation was celebrated; adding, at the same time, the most fearful maledictions against perjury. Alphonso never forgave the liberty thus taken with him, and soon after banished the Spanish hero from court, under pretence of his having trespassed on the territories of an ally of Castile, the King of Toledo, into whose dominions the Cid had inadvertently pursued some fugitives from justice.

The period of his exile became the most glorious epoch in the history of the Chevalier de Bivar: it was then that he achieved so many triumphs over the Moors, aided solely by the brave companions in arms whom his reputation drew to his standard. After a time Alphonso recalled the Cid, and received him into apparent favour; but Rodrigue was too candid long to enjoy the royal smiles. Banished from court anew, he hastened to accomplish the conquest of Valencia; and master of that strong city, with many others, and of a territory of great extent, to make the Cid a monarch it was only necessary that he himself should desire it. But the noble Spaniard never for a moment indulged the wish, and ever continued the faithful subject of the ungrateful and often-offending Alphonso.

This celebrated hero died at Valencia A.D. 1099, crowned with years and honours. He had but one son, and of him he was early deprived by death. The two daughters of the Cid espoused princes of the house of Navarre; and, through a long succession of alliances, formed at length the root whence is derived the present royal race of Bourbons.

C, page 92.

More ferocious and sanguinary than the lions of their deserts,
&c.

The history of Africa, during the period referred to in the text, is but a narrative of one continued succession of the most atrocious murders. Were we to judge of humanity by these sanguinary annals, we should be tempted to believe, that, of all ferocious animals, man is the most bloodthirsty and cruel.

Amid the multitude of these African tyrants, there was one, of the race of the *Aglhebites*, named *Abon Ishak*, who was particularly distinguished for the demoniac barbarity of his character. Having butchered eight of his brothers, he next indulged his horrid thirst for blood in the sacrifice of his own offspring. The mother of this monster succeeded with difficulty in preserving from his fury a part of his family. One day, while dining with Ishak, upon his expressing some feeling of momentary regret that he had no more children, his mother tremblingly ventured to confess that she had preserved the lives of six of his daughters. The sanguinary wretch appeared softened, and expressed a desire to see them. When they were summoned to his presence, their youth and loveliness touched the ferocious father; and while Ishak lavished caresses upon his innocent children, his mother retired, with tears of joy, to render thanks to Heaven for this apparent change in the temper of her son. An hour afterward, a eunuch brought her, by order of the emperor, the heads of the young princesses.

It would be easy to cite other parallel deeds, attested by historians, which were perpetrated by this execrable monster. Suffice it to say, he escaped the violent death due to such a life, and long maintained his hateful rule.

Time has not softened the sanguinary ferocity, which seems like an inherent vice produced by the climate of Africa. Mulci-Abdalla, the father of Sidi Mohammed, the recent king of Morocco, renewed these scenes of horror. One day, while crossing a river, he was on the point of drowning, when one of his negroes succeeded in rescuing him from the waves. The slave expressed his delight at having had the good fortune to serve his master. His words were heard by Abdalla, who, drawing his cimeter, and crying, " Behold an infidel, who supposes that God required his assistance in preserving the life of an emperor," instantly struck off the head of his preserver.

This same monarch had a confidential domestic who had been long in his service, and for whom the savage Abdalla appeared to entertain some affection. In a moment of good-nature he entreated this aged servant to accept two thousand ducats at his hand and leave his service, lest he should be seized with an irrepressible desire to kill him, as he had so many others. The old man clung to the feet of the king, refused the two thousand ducats, and assured him that he preferred perishing by his hand rather than abandon so beloved a master. Mulei, with some hesitation, consented to retain his aged servant. Some days afterward, impelled by that thirst for blood whose impulses were sometimes uncontrollable, and without the slightest provocation to the deed, the fiendish despot struck the unfortunate man dead at his feet, saying, at the same moment, that he had been a fool not to accept his permission to leave him.

It is painful to relate these shocking details; but they present a true picture of the character of these African sovereigns, while they inspire us with a horror of tyranny, and a veneration for the restraints of civilization and law, so indispensable to the well-being of every community.

D, page 98.

And possessed the united glory of having both enlightened, &c

Averroes belonged to one of the first families in Cordova. His version of the writings of Aristotle was translated into Latin, and was for a long time the only translation of the works of that author. The other productions of Averroes are still esteemed by the learned. He is justly regarded as the chief of the Arabic philosophers: a class of men not numerous in a nation abounding in prophets and conquerors. The principles he entertained exposed him to much persecution. His indifference to the religious creed of his countrymen excited the enmity of the imans or priests against him, and afforded a pretext for the animosity of all whom his genius inspired with envy. He was accused of heresy before the Emperor of Morocco; and the punishment decreed against him was, that he should do homage at the door of the mosque, while every true Mussulman who came thither to pray for his conversion should spit in his face. He submitted patiently to the humiliating infliction, merely repeating the words *Moriatur anima mea morte philosophorum* (*Let me die the death of a philosopher*).

E, page 106.

And broke the chains, &c.

This King of Navarre was Sancho VIII., surnamed *the Strong*. It was in commemoration of the chains broken by him at the battle of Toloza that Sancho added the chains of gold to the arms of Navarre, which are still to be seen on the field of gules.

F, page 111.

Cousin-german of St. Lewis, &c.

Blanche, the mother of St. Lewis, was the daughter of Alphonso the Noble of Castile. She had a sister named Beringira, who became the wife of the King of Leon, and the mother of Ferdinand III. Several historians, among others Mariana and Garibai, maintain that Blanche was older than Beringira. If it were so, St. Lewis was the rightful heir to the throne of Castile. France long asserted the pretensions thus created. It is surprising that historians have not settled this disputed point. One thing, however, is certain: the claims of Ferdinand, sustained as they were by the partiality of the Castilians, prevailed over those of his cousin.

FOURTH EPOCH.

A, page 132.

Alphonso the Sage, &c.

Alphonso the Sage was a great astronomer: his *Alphonsine Tables* prove that the happiness of his people occupied his attention as much, at least, as his literary pursuits. It is in this collection that this remarkable sentence occurs—remarkable when it is considered that it expresses the sentiments of a monarch of the thirteenth century : *"The despot uproots the tree: the wise sovereign prunes it."*

B, page 135.

In the hope of being elected emperor, &c.

ALPHONSO THE SAGE was elected Emperor of Germany in the year twelve hundred and fifty-seven : but he was at too great a distance from that country, and too much occupied at home, to be able to support his claims to the imperial throne. Sixteen years afterward, however, he made a voyage to Lyons, where Pope Gregory X. then was, to advocate his rights before that dignitary. But the sovereign pontiff decided in favour of Rodolph of Hapsburg, a scion of the house of Austria.

C, page 136.

Sancho reigned in his father's stead, &c.

This Sancho, surnamed *the Brave,* who took up arms against his father and afterward obtained his throne, was the second son of Alphonso the Sage. His elder brother, Ferdinand de la Cerda, a mild and virtuous prince, died in the flower of his age, leaving two infant sons, the offspring of his marriage with Blanche, the daughter of St. Lewis of France. It was to deprive these children of their reversionary right to the crown of Castile that the ambitious Sancho made war upon his father. He succeeded in his criminal designs; but the princes of La Cerda, protected by France and Aragon, rallied around them all the malecontents of Castile, and the claims they were thus enabled to support long formed a pretext or occasion for the most bloody dissensions.

D, page 149.
Ferdinand IV., surnamed the Summoned, &c.

Ferdinand IV., the son and successor of Sancho the Brave, was still in his infancy when he succeeded to the throne. His minority was overshadowed by impending clouds; but the power and influence of Queen Mary, his mother, enabled her eventually to dissipate the dangers which threatened the safety of her son. This prince obtained his appellation of *the Summoned* from the following circumstance. Actuated by feelings of strong indignation, Ferdinand commanded that two brothers, named Carvajal, who had been accused, but not convicted, of the crime of assassination, should be precipitated from a rocky precipice. Both the supposed criminals, in their last moments, asserted their innocence of the crime alleged against them, appealed to Heaven and the laws to verify the truth of their protestations, and *summoned* the passionate Ferdinand to appear before the Great Judge of all men at the end of thirty days. At the precise time thus indicated, the Castilian king, who was marching against the Moors, retired for repose after dinner, and was found dead upon his couch. The Spaniards attributed this sudden death to the effects of Divine justice. It had been well if the monarchs who succeeded Ferdinand, Peter the Cruel in particular, had been convinced of the truth of this sentiment.

E, page 149.

Retiring within the walls of Tariffe, &c.

After Sancho the Brave became master of Tariffe, it was besieged by the Africans. It was during this siege that Alphonso de Guzman, the Spanish governor of the city, exhibited an example of invincible firmness and self-command, of which none but parents can form a just estimate. The son of De Guzman was taken prisoner during a sortie. The Africans conducted their captive to the walls, and threatened the governor with his immolation unless the city should be immediately surrendered. The undaunted Spaniard replied only by hurling a poniard at his enemies, and retired from the battlements. In a moment loud cries burst from the garrison. Hastily demanding the cause of this alarm, the unhappy father was told that the Africans had put to death his son. "God be praised," said he, " I thought that the city had been taken!"

F, page 158.

The celebrated Inez de Castro, &c.

The passion of Peter the Cruel for Inez de Castro was carried to such excess as, perhaps, in some degree, to account for the atrocity of his revenge upon her murderers. These were three distinguished Portuguese lords, who themselves stabbed the unfortunate Inez in the arms of her women. Peter, who, at the time this barbarous deed was committed, had not yet attained regal power, seemed from that period to lose all command of himself : from being gentle and virtuous, he became ferocious and almost insane. He openly rebelled against his father, carried fire and sword into those parts of the kingdom in which the domains of the assassins of Inez were situated, and, when he afterward came into possession of the crown, insisted that the King of Castile should deliver up Gonzales and Coello, two of the guilty noblemen, who had taken refuge at his court. Thus master of the persons of two of his victims (the third had fled into France, where he died), Peter subjected them to the most dreadful tortures. He caused their hearts to be torn out while they were yet living, and assisted himself at this horrible sacrifice. After thus glutting his vengeance, the inconsolable lover exhumed the body of his murdered mistress, clothed it in magnificent habiliments, and, placing his crown upon the livid and revolting brow, proclaimed Inez de Castro queen of Portugal; compelling, at the same time, the grandees of his court to do homage to the insensible remains which he had invested with the attributes of royalty.

G, page 161.

Most of the productions of the Grenadian authors, &c.

After the surrender of Grenada, Cardinal Ximenes caused every copy of the Koran of which he could obtain possession to be burned. The ignorant and superstitious soldiery mistook for that work everything written in the Arabic language, and committed to the flames a multitude of compositions both in prose and verse.

H, page 178.

The Abencerrages, &c.

The inhabitants of Grenada, and, indeed, the whole Moorish people, were divided into tribes, composed of the different branches of the same family. Some of these tribes were more numerous and important than others: but two distinct races were never united together, nor was one of them ever divided. At the head of each of these tribes was a chief who was descended in a direct male line from the original founder of the family. In the city of Grenada there existed thirty-two considerable tribes. The most important of these were the Abencerrages, the Zegris, the Alcenabez, the Almorades, the Vanegas, the Gomeles, the Abidbars, the Gauzuls, the Abenamars, the Aliatars, the Reduans, the Aldoradins, etc. These separate races were, many of them, at enmity with each other; and their animosity being perpetuated from one generation to another, gave rise to the frequent civil wars which were attended with such disastrous consequences to the nation at large.

I, page 198

His humane injunctions respecting almsgiving, &c.

Almsgiving is one of the leading principles of the Mohammedan religion. It was enjoined upon the followers of the Prophet by a variety of allegories, among which is the following: "The sovereign Judge shall, at the last great day, entwine him who has not bestowed alms with a frightful serpent, whose envenomed sting shall for ever pierce the avaricious hand that never opened for the relief of the unfortunate!"

A BRIEF ACCOUNT

OF THE

RISE AND DECLINE

OF THE

MOHAMMEDAN EMPIRE;

THE LITERATURE, SCIENCE, AND RELIGION OF THE
ARABS; AND THE PRESENT CONDITION OF
MOHAMMEDANISM.

A BRIEF ACCOUNT

OF THE

MOHAMMEDAN EMPIRE.

CHAPTER I.

Extent of the Arabian Empire.—Causes which led to that extent.—Continuance of Mohammedanism.—Decay of the Empire.—What led to it.—Spain revolts and sets up a separate Caliph.—Africa.—Egypt.—Bagdad.—Fall of the House of the Abbassides.

THE first battle in which the Arabs tried their power against the disciplined forces of the Roman empire was the battle of Muta. Though on that occasion they were successful, the most sanguine could not have ventured to predict that, before the close of a century, their empire would become more extensive than any that had ever before existed. Yet such was the fact. It overthrew the power of the Romans, and rendered the successors of the Prophet the mightiest and most absolute sovereigns on earth.

Under the last monarch of the Ommiade race,

the Arabian empire, excepting only an obscure part of Africa, of little account, embraced a compact territory equal to six months' march of a caravan in length and four in breadth, with innumerable tributary and dependant states. In the exercise of their power, the caliphs were fettered neither by popular rights, the votes of a senate, nor constitutional laws: the Koran was, indeed, their professed rule of action; but, inasmuch as they alone were its interpreters, their will was in all cases law. The loss of Spain to the empire was more than made up by conquests in India, Tartary, and European Turkey. Samarcand and Timbuctoo studied with equal devotion the language and religion of the Koran, and at the temple of Mecca the Moor and the Indian met as brother pilgrims. Throughout the countries west of the Tigris, the language of Arabia became the vehicle of popular intercourse; and, although in Persia, Tartary, and Hindostan the native dialects continued in common use, the Arabic was also there the sacred tongue.

We will advert to some of the causes which led to this astonishing success. The leading article of the Mohammedan faith, the unity of God, harmonized with what Jews and Christians universally believed. Mohammed propounded this doctrine, by excluding the Deity of Jesus Christ, so as to fall in with the views of the greater number of the Christian sectaries. He moreover enjoined practices which, in the then corrupt state of religion, were beginning widely to prevail. To the untutored mind of the desert wanderer, his doctrine would thus possess all the attractiveness he might have heard ascribed to Christianity, while his being of the same country would secure for him the greater attention. Systems in which truth and error have been combined are by no means unwillingly received, especially by those who are already superstitious and fanatical, and such was pre-eminently the character of the Arabians. Mohammed's religious, moral, and juridical system was in general accordance with Asiatic opinions; it provided a paradise exactly suited to the imagination and taste of the Orientals; and, as the superstitious are always more powerfully influenced by that which awakens apprehension and appeals to fear than by what enkindles hope, his hell contributed even more than his heaven to multiply disciples.

Still, had no resort been had to arms, the Mohammedan faith would in all probability have been confined to the deserts of Arabia. The whole of Asia was at that time in a state of unprecedented military inactivity, and opportunity was thus afforded for the success of his enterprise. Empires were tottering and powerless; political wisdom had almost disappeared; and to military talents and courage the Arabs alone could make any pretensions. Previous contentions between the Persian and Byzantine empires had entirely destroyed what little remains of internal vigour those governments might otherwise have possessed. Civil revolts, tyranny, extortion, sensuality, and sloth, had annihilated the ambition of universal rule which the Greek and Roman governments had once cherished; and their provinces, neglected or oppressed, became an easy prey to the Moslem power.

The nations were the more rapidly subdued, since to the indomitable ferocity of the desert wanderer the Saracens added those other features which complete a warlike character. They despised death, and were self-denying and energetic to a degree far beyond the soldiers of civilized countries, while they were scarcely less familiar with the military art. The lieutenants of the caliphs soon vied with the Roman generals in skill; and it is by no means difficult to explain their almost uniform superiority, when we bear in mind the character of the armies they respectively commanded. Terror, moreover, is epidemic; and a force already successful commonly finds its victorious progress greatly aided by the prevailing notion of its prowess. Thus we have witnessed, in the wars of more disciplined troops, the tremendous effect of a name alone.

It may be added, also, that the Saracen success is greatly attributable to that ardent and impetuous spirit of religious enthusiasm with which they fought. They deemed their cause the cause of God; heaven, they were persuaded, was engaged in their behalf; every one who fell in their wars was a martyr; and cowardice was tantamount to apostacy.

The religious ardour of the Crusaders, in the eleventh and twelfth centuries, to exterminate Mohammedanism, did not exceed, if it even equalled, that of the Arab soldiers by whom that system had been originally propagated. Whatever secular principles and ambition influenced them, they took credit for fighting in the support of truth and virtue. The sword and the Koran were equally the companions and the instruments of their wars. "The circumstance," says Paley, in his admirable exhibition of the Evidences of Christianity,* "that Mohammed's conquests should carry his religion along with them, will excite little surprise when we know the conditions which he proposed to the vanquished: death or conversion was the only choice offered to idolators. To the Jews and Christians was left the somewhat milder alterna-

* Vol. ii., § 3.

tive of subjection and tribute if they persisted in their own religion, or of an equal participation of the rights and liberties, the honours and privileges of the faithful if they embraced the religion of their conquerors."

Literature, in the days of Mohammed, was as little regarded as was pure and practical Christianity. His followers everywhere met with an ignorant and easily-deluded people. Both the monuments of science and the means of freedom had been abolished by the barbarians of the North. Philosophy and the liberal arts found no patrons among indolent and luxurious emperors and nobles. Superstition, therefore, naturally took possession of the minds of men, and, as neither fears nor hopes were moderated by knowledge, idle, preposterous, and unnecessary ceremonies easily obtained currency. Mohammed merely changed one set of ceremonies for another; and in this there was little difficulty, since, in the almost universal darkness of mankind, terror and credulity everywhere prevailed.

The continuance of the religion of Mohammed in countries after the Arab dominion over them had ceased, may be also easily accounted for. "Everything in Asia is a matter of regulation; and freedom of opinion being but little permitted or encouraged in the despotic governments of the

East, Mohammedanism, when once received, became stationary. The human code is mingled with the divine, and the ideas of change and profanation are inseparable. As the unsettling of the political and social fabric might ensue from a change of modes of faith, all classes of men are interested in preserving the national religion."* Besides this, in their own nature religious doctrines are more permanent in their hold than forms of civil government: it may be questioned, for instance, whether, whatever civil changes Scotland might undergo, Presbyterianism would ever cease to be the prevalent faith of its inhabitants. A people may, with the overthrow of usurped civil power, return to their ancient religion, whatever it is: but when once a religion has become, so to speak, indigenous, it is likely to be permanent. Such is the religion of the Koran both in Asia and Africa.

The elements of political weakness and decay soon began to be developed in the chief seat of the Saracen empire. In the earliest days of the caliphate, after the accession of the Ommiade dynasty, the princes of Damascus were regarded as the heads of the Moslem faith; while the governors of Arabia successively obtained, as to civil rule, their independence. To this the widely-extended wars in which the caliphs were engaged no doubt con-

* Mills, p. 179.

tributed. Other provinces followed the example; and, as the empire enlarged, the remoteness and degeneracy of the Syrian court encouraged the governors to assume to themselves everything except the name of king, and to render their dignities hereditary. All the provinces were nominally connected with the empire by the payment of tribute; but means were easily devised to withhold this, under pretence of prosecuting the wars of the caliph, though really to strengthen his rebellious deputies against him. If in this we discover a want of efficiency in the government, we need not be surprised: the systems of the Macedonian hero and of the Roman conquerors were equally defective; and perhaps we should attribute such deficiency to a wise and beneficent arrangement of Providence, which, that oppression may never become permanent and universal, permits not any empire for a very long time to hold dominion over countries dissimilar in their habits and character, and independent of each other.

To the establishment of these separate states, the luxury and effeminacy of the court at Damascus in no small degree contributed. In the early periods of the caliphate, simplicity and charity chiefly distinguished their rulers; but, as the wealth and power of the Saracens increased, they imitated the splendour and magnificence of the monarchs of Persia and Greece. Abulfeda says of the court in the year 917: "The Caliph Moctadi's whole army, both horse and foot, were under arms, which together made a body of one hundred and sixty thousand men. His state officers stood near him in the most splendid apparel, their belts shining with gold and gems. Near them were seven thousand black and white eunuchs. The porters or doorkeepers were in number seven hundred. Barges and boats, with the most superb decorations, were swimming on the Tigris. Nor was the palace itself less splendid, in which were hung thirty-eight thousand pieces of tapestry, twelve thousand five hundred of which were of silk embroidered with gold. The carpets on the floor were twenty-two thousand. A hundred lions were brought out, with a keeper to each lion. Among the other spectacles of rare and stupendous luxury was a tree of gold and silver, which opened itself into eighteen larger branches, upon which and the other smaller branches sat birds of every sort, made also of gold and silver. The tree glittered with leaves of the same metals; and while its branches, through machinery, appeared to move of themselves, the several birds upon them warbled their natural notes."

When, moreover, decline had once commenced, its progress was accelerated by the means taken to arrest it. After the regular troops had been corrupted by faction, the caliphs, for the defence of their person and government, formed a militia; but the soldiers composing this force, not unfrequently foreigners, soon governed with a military despotism similar to that of the janizaries of Turkey, the Mamelukes of Egypt, or the prætorian guards of Rome; and, in addition to these causes of decay, a furious spirit of sectarianism tore asunder the very strength and heart of the empire. The colossal power of the successors of Mohammed, suddenly towering to its awful height, almost as suddenly fell, as if to yield more perfect confirmation of the truth, that all earthly things are destined to pass away, while the word of the living God abideth for ever.

Spain, as has been seen, was the first distant province of the Arabian empire which succeeded in separating itself and setting up an independent caliph. As this country had been brought under the Moslem yoke by means chiefly furnished from the northern states of Africa, its independence was likely to produce a corresponding effect upon those states. They were governed in the name of the Bagdad caliphs; but for nearly a century they had been growing into independence, under rulers usually known, from the name of their progenitor, as the Aglabite dynasty. Early in the ninth century, the throne of Mauritania, Massilia, and Carthage was seized by Obeidollah, whose successors assumed the title of Mihidi, or directors of the faithful. The districts of Fez and Tangiers, which had been already wrested from the princes of Bagdad by the real or pretended posterity of Ali, were soon brought under his dominion; and, before the end of the tenth century, all acknowledgment of the Abbassidan rule was obliterated by the suppression of public prayers for the princes of that race. A succession of changes distracted the country for some five centuries afterward; but, about the year 1516, the descendants of Mohammed were raised to the throne of Morocco, which has been transmitted, without interruption, in the same line, to its present possessors. Moez, the last of the African princes of the house of Obeidollah, who seems to have depended for his dominion more on his prowess than on his supposed descent from Mohammed,* transferred his court to Grand Cairo, a city which he had built in Egypt after his conquest of that country. Africa was to be held as a fief of this new empire. Large tracts of Syria and the whole of Palestine acknowledged the

* When it was demanded of Moez from what branch of Mohammed's family he drew his title, "This," said he, showing his cimeter, "is my pedigree; and these," throwing gold among his soldiers, "are my children."

supremacy of his descendants, commonly known as Fatimites, from their supposed relationship to Ali, and to Fatima, the Prophet's daughter. They possessed also the sovereignty of the Holy Land: against them, therefore, the crusades of Europe were chiefly directed. During these formidable wars the caliphs of Egypt sought assistance from those of Bagdad; and Noureddin, a prince of that empire, protected them against their Western assailants. The weakness of Egypt, however, came thus to be known to the crafty and powerful caliphs of Bagdad, and in a short time its Asiatic dominions were seized upon by Noureddin and Saladin. As Adhed, the last caliph of Egypt, was dying in the mosque of Cairo, these generals proclaimed Morthadi, the thirty-third caliph of Bagdad, as his successor. Saladin, whose name, from his activity, courage, and success against the crusaders, is better known to the readers of European history than that of almost any other Mohammedan prince, soon made himself master of Egypt; but his successors could not maintain the power he had acquired. The country is now governed by the celebrated Mohammed Ali, nominally as viceroy of the Turkish emperor, though he is in reality a sovereign and independent prince.

The caliphs of the house of Abbas, having built the city of Bagdad soon after their accession to the throne, transferred thither their court and the seat of power. For five centuries they reigned there with various degrees of authority; but foreign wars and domestic revolts gradually dissolved the empire, and their dominion at length passed away. Radhi, the twentieth caliph of the race, was "the last," says Abulfeda, " who harangued the people from the pulpit; who passed the cheerful hour of leisure with men of learning and taste; whose expenses, resources, and treasures, whose table and magnificence, had any resemblance to those of the ancient caliphs." "During the next three centuries," says a modern historian of the Arabian empire, " the successors of Mohammed swayed a feeble sceptre. Sometimes their state was so degraded that they were confined in their palaces like prisoners, and occasionally were almost reduced to the want of corporeal subsistence. The tragic scenes of fallen royalty at length were closed; for, towards the middle of the seventh century of the Hegira, the metropolis of Islamism fell into the hands of Houlagou Khan, the grandson of Zenghis Khan, and emperor of the Moguls and Tartars, who reigned at that period with absolute and unmixed despotism over every nation of the East. The caliph Mostasem, the thirty-seventh of his house, was murdered under circumstances of peculiar barbarity, and the caliphate of Bagdad expired. Though the dignity and sovereignty of the caliphs were lost by this fatal event, and the soul which animated the form had fled, yet the name existed for three centuries longer in the eighteen descendants of Mostanser Billah, a son, or pretended son, of Daker, the last but one of this race of princes.

"Mostanser Billah and his successors, to the number of eighteen, were called the second dynasty of the Abbassides, and were spiritual chiefs of the Mohammedan religion, but without the slightest vestige of temporal authority. When Selim, emperor of the Turks, conquered Egypt and destroyed the power of the Mamelukes, he carried the caliph, whom he found there a prisoner, to Constantinople, and accepted from him a renunciation of his ecclesiastical supremacy. On the death of the caliph, the family of the Abbassides, once so illustrious, and which had borne the title of caliph for almost eight hundred years, sunk with him from obscurity into oblivion."*

* Mill's History, 160.

CHAPTER II.

Literature and Science of the Arabs.—Their Facilities for Literary and Scientific Pursuits.—Patronage of Literature by the Princes of the House of Abbas.—Almamoun.—Arabian Schools.—Eloquence.—Poetry.—The Arabian Tales.—History.—Geography.—Speculative Sciences.—Astrology.—Mathematical Knowledge of the Arabs.—Astronomy.—Architecture.—The Fine Arts.—Agriculture.—Medicine.—Chymistry.—Our obligations to Arab Literature.

THE early followers of the Arabian prophet were only enthusiastic military adventurers, subduing in their wide and rapid progress most of the nations of the then known world. The lust of power, and successful military enterprise, are commonly unfavourable to the cultivation of the liberal arts, so that a conquering people usually exhibit but little taste for science or literature. The Goths and the Huns, for instance, were among the most implacable foes of knowledge. Nor did the early Arabs regard it with more favour. Mohammed found his countrymen sunk in the deepest barbarism: he was incapable of any direct effort to raise them; and, from the ruthless destruction of the Alexandrean library by Omar, one of his earliest successors, they appear not to have been in a much better condition after the close than at the commencement of his eventful career.

Their settlement in the countries they had subdued, the unlimited resources which their widespread conquests placed within their reach, and probably the leisure which their almost universal dominion afforded, speedily led to a change in their character in relation to literary pursuits, of which the more enlightened nations of the West are still reaping the advantage. It was about the middle of the seventh century that Omar committed the famous library of Alexandrea to the flames: before the end of the eighth, literature began to enjoy the munificent patronage of the caliphs of the Abbassidan race, who superinduced upon the stern fanaticism of the followers of the Prophet the softening influences of learning; and, by an anomaly in the history of mankind, the most valuable lessons in science and the arts have been received from a people who pursued with relentless hostility the religion and liberties of every other nation.

The Greeks were the most distinguished patrons of literature and science. Among them philosophy found its earliest home, and the arts are commonly supposed to have sprung up chiefly under their fostering care, though modern researches have shown that much of their knowledge was derived from still more ancient sources. Their philosophy, though greatly improved by them, was borrowed from the mysteries of the Egyptian priests and the Persian magi. Their system of the universe, which made the nearest approach to the more correct discoveries of modern times, was previously known to the learned Hindus; and it may admit of question whether their whole mythology, allowing for the additions which a chastened and vivid imagination would make to it, had not its prototype in some Asiatic religio-philosophical system. A learned writer on the erudition of the Asiatics says, that the whole of the theology of the Greeks, and part of the philosophy of modern scientific research, may be found in the Hindu Vedas. He adds, " That most subtile spirit which Newton suspected to pervade natural bodies, and to lie concealed in them so as to cause attraction and repulsion, the emission, reflection, and refraction of light, electrictiy, calefaction, sensation, and muscular motion, is described by the Hindus as a fifth element, endued with those very powers; and the Vedas abound with allusions to a force universally attractive, which they chiefly attribute to the sun." The extension, therefore, of the Arabian victories over the Eastern world, and their entire command, after the overthrow of the Greek empire, of the resources possessed by that people, gave them access to all the literary stores then in existence.

It has been said, and probably not without good reason, that Mohammed himself saw and felt the importance of literary distinction. Among the sayings attributed to him, the following has been considered as evincing his sense of the value of learning: "A mind without erudition is like a body without a soul. Glory consists not in wealth, but in knowledge;" and, as the Koran affords abundant proof, he was by no means unmindful of that mental cultivation, of which the means were within his reach. His immediate followers, occupied only with the ideas of conquest and conversion, despised equally the religion and learning of the nations they subdued; but when the age of rapine and violence yielded at length to comparative security and quiet, and the fair and splendid city of the Oriental caliphs arose, the Muses were courted from their ancient temples, and by the milder and more graceful achievements of literature and science, efforts were made to expiate the guilt of former conquest, and to shed a purer lustre over the Mohammedan name.

Almansor, the second of the dynasty of the Abbassides, whose reign commenced A.D. 754, and lasted twenty-one years, was among the first of the Arab princes to foster learning and the arts. Jurisprudence and astronomy were the principal subjects of his study, which, however, through the instruction of a Greek physician in his court, he extended to the art of healing, and probably to those kindred arts with which, in all ages and countries, medical science has been connected. What progress was made by himself or his subjects, we cannot now ascertain. His two immediate successors seem not to have trodden in his steps, though it is probable they did not undo what he had done; for the next caliph, Haroun al Raschid, is renowned as one of the most munificent patrons that literature ever enjoyed. He was fond of poetry and music: he is said to have constantly surrounded himself with a great number of learned men; and to him the Arabs were deeply indebted for the progress in knowledge which they were enabled to make. Every mosque in his dominions had a school attached to it by his order; and, as if his love of learning were superior even to his hereditary faith, he readily tolerated men of science who refused to yield to the bold pretensions of the Prophet. A Nestorian Christian presided over his schools, and directed the academical studies of his subjects. His successor imitated his wise and generous course; and thus knowledge extended from the capital to the most distant extremities of the empire.

But it was during the reign of Almamoun, the seventh of the Abbassidan princes, A.D. 813–833, that literature flourished most among the Arabs. Learned men, professors of the Christian faith, had multiplied at Bagdad under the tolerant reigns of his predecessors, and they were now liberally encouraged to unfold their ample stores of knowledge. The copious language of Arabia was employed to communicate whatever that of the Greeks had hitherto concealed, though, with a barbarism for which it is difficult to account, many of the original works were destroyed as soon as translations of them were made. Almamoun in his youth had associated with the most eminent scholars of Greece, Persia, and Chaldea; and he now invited them to his court. Bagdad was resorted to by poets, philosophers, and mathematicians, from every country and of every creed. Armenia, Syria, and Egypt were explored by his agents for literary treasures, which were amassed with infinite care, and presented at the foot of the throne as the richest and most acceptable tribute that conquered provinces could render. Camels, hitherto employed exclusively in traffic, were seen entering the royal city laden with Hebrew, Persian, and Grecian manuscripts. The court assumed the appearance rather of an academy than of a council guiding the affairs of a luxurious and warlike government, and all classes were encouraged to apply themselves to the acquisition of knowledge with a zeal commensurate to the advantages thus afforded. "I chose," said Almamoun, when remonstrated with for appointing a learned Christian to an office of no small influence over the intellectual pursuits of his people, "I chose this learned man, not to be my guide in religious affairs, but to be my teacher of science; and it is well known that the wisest men are to be found among the Jews and Christians."*

Under such favourable auspices, it is not to be wondered at that the Saracens became a literary people. The caliphs of the West and of Africa imitated their brethren of the East. "At one period, six thousand professors and pupils cultivated liberal studies in the college of Bagdad. Twenty schools made Grand Cairo a chief seat of letters; and the talents of the students were exercised in the perusal of the royal library, which consisted of one hundred thousand manuscripts. The African writers dwell with pride and satisfaction on the literary institutions which adorned the towns on the northern coast of their sandy plain. The sun of science arose even in Africa, and the manners of the Moorish savage were softened by philosophy.

* Abulferage, p. 160.

Their brethren in Europe amassed numerous and magnificent collections; two hundred and eighty thousand volumes were in Cordova, and more than seventy libraries were open to public curiosity in the kingdom of Andalusia."

We know but little of the internal government of the Arabian schools, or of the studies actually pursued. Aristotle, no doubt, was the great master to whom, in philosophy, all deference was paid. The Prophet had prescribed their religion. Their schools were of two kinds, or rather classes; the one comprehending the inferior institutions, in which elementary branches of instruction, such as reading, writing, and religious doctrine were chiefly attended to; the other, called *Madras*, mostly connected with the mosques, as were all the schools of the former class, included those institutions in which the higher departments of knowledge were explored. Here grammar, logic, theology, and jurisprudence were studied. The management of each school was confided to a principal of known ability, and not always a Mohammedan. The professors lectured on the several sciences; and the pupils, if not in every department, of which there is some doubt, certainly in that of medicine, were publicly examined, and diplomas were given under the hand of the chief physician.

Of elegant composition, the Koran was universally esteemed the model. Hence it was studied with the most diligent care by all who sought to distinguish themselves in the art of eloquence, one of the leading acquirements of Arab scholars. Subordinate to this pre-eminent composition, their schools of oratory boasted of models scarcely inferior to the celebrated orators of antiquity. Malek and Sharaif, the one for pathos, the other for brilliancy, are the chief of these. Horaiai was esteemed as the compeer of Demosthenes and Cicero. Bedreddin, of Grenada, was their "torch of eloquence;" and Sekaki obtained the honourable designation of the Arabian Quinctilian.

The ancient Arabs were much inclined to poetry. The wild, romantic scenery of the land they inhabited, the sacred recollections of their earliest history, the life they led, everything around them, contributed to poetic inspiration. After the revival of letters, this art was cultivated with enthusiasm. The heroic measures of Ferdousi, the didactic verses of Sadi, and the lyric strains of Hafiz, even through the medium of imperfect translations, discover animated descriptions, bold metaphors, and striking expressions, that at once delight and surprise us. In splendour, if not in strength, the poets of the courts of Haroun and Almamoun, or those of the Ommiades of Spain, have, perhaps, in no age been excelled. In this art, as among other people, so among the Arabs, the fair sex have distinguished themselves. Valadata, Aysha, Labana, Safia, and others, have obtained the highest encomiums.

So great is the number of Arabian poets, that Abul Abbas, a son of Motassem, who wrote an abridgment of their lives in the ninth century, numbers one hundred and thirty. Other authors have occupied twenty-four, thirty, and one no less than fifty volumes, in recording their history.

The Arabs, however, are entirely without epic poetry, so important a department of the art; nor have they anything that may be properly ranked as dramatic composition. Sophocles, Euripides, Terence, and Seneca, the classic models of Greece and Rome, they despised as timid, constrained, and cold; and under whatever obligation to these ancient nations the Arabs may have been in other departments of literature, they owe them nothing, or next to nothing, in this. Their poetry was original and local; their figures and comparisons were strictly their own. To understand and properly appreciate them, we must have a knowledge of the productions of their country, and of the character, institutions, and manners of its inhabitants. The muse delights in illustrations and figures borrowed from pastoral life; that of Judea revels among the roses of Sharon, the verdant slopes of

Carmel, and the glory of Lebanon; while the Arab muse selects for her ornaments the pearls of Omar, the musk of Hadramaut, the groves and nightingales of Aden, and the spicy odours of Yemen. If these appear to us fantastic, it must be remembered they are borrowed from objects and scenes to which we are almost utter strangers.

Who is not familiar with the Alif lita wa lilin, or the thousand and one tales, commonly known as the Arabian Nights' Entertainment? Some have questioned whether they are an original work, or a translation from the Indian or Persian, made in the Augustan age of Arab literature: a doubt certainly not warranted by any want of exactness in their description of Arabian life and manners. They seem to have been originally the legends of itinerant story-tellers, a class of persons still very numerous in every part of the Mohammedan world. The scenes they unfold, true to nature; the simplicity displayed in their characters, their beauty and their moral instruction, appeal irresistibly to the hearts of all; while the learned concede to them the merit of more perfectly describing the manners of the singular people from whom they sprung, than the works of any traveller, however accomplished and indefatigable.

Of history the ancient Arabs were strangely negligent; but, by the more modern, this department of knowledge has been cultivated with greater care and success. Annals, chronicles, and memoirs, almost numberless, are extant among them: kingdoms, provinces, and towns are described, and their history is narrated in volumes, a bare catalogue of which would extend to a wearisome length. They abound, however, more in the fanciful than in the substantial and correct. Of this, the titles of some of the most approved works of this kind may be taken as specimens: A Chronology of the Caliphs of Spain and Africa is denominated "A Silken Vest, embroidered with the Needle;" a History of Grenada, "A Specimen of the Full Moon;" Ibn Abbas and Abu Bakri are authors of historical collections, entitled respectively, "Mines of Silver," and "Pearls and picked-up Flowers." Yet some of their writers, as Ibn Katibi, are chiefly remarkable for the extent and accuracy of their historical knowledge; and some of their works are exceedingly voluminous. A full history of Spain occupied six authors in succession, and cost the labour of one hundred and fifteen years to complete. Their biography was not confined to men. Ibn Zaid and Abul Mondar wrote a genealogical history of distinguished horses; and Alasucco and Abdolmalec performed the same service for camels worthy of being had in remembrance. Encyclopædias and gazetteers, with dictionaries of the sciences and other similar works, occupied Arabian pens long before they came into vogue among more modern literati. Every species of composition, indeed, and almost every subject, in one age or another, have engaged the attention of learned Mohammedans.

Geography they did not so well understand, their means of acquiring knowledge on this subject being exceedingly limited. Yet their public libraries could boast of globes, voyages, and itineraries, the productions of men who travelled to acquire geographical information. With statistics and political economy they had but an imperfect acquaintance; yet so early as the reign of Omar II. we find a work devoted to these subjects, giving an account of the provinces and cities of Spain, with its rivers, ports, and harbours; of the climate, soil, mountains, plants, and minerals of that country; with its imports, and the manner in which its several productions, natural and artificial, might be manufactured and applied to the best advantage. Money, weights, and measures, with whatever else political economy may be understood to include, were also subjects which employed their ingenious speculations, and, in some cases, their laborious research.

The speculative sciences, scarcely less than polite literature, flourished among the Arabs. Indeed, what superstitious, enthusiastic people has ever neglected these? Their ardour in the more dignified of these pursuits was badly regulated; subtleties were preferred to important practical truths; and, frequently, the more ingenious the sophism, constructed after the rules of Aristotle, the more welcome was it to men who rendered to that philosopher a homage almost idolatrous. The later Arabs, and the Turks of the present day, pay no little attention to astrology, though it is strongly prohibited by their Prophet. This science was universally employed by the idolaters, against whom his denunciations are scarcely less inveterate than are those of the inspired volume; and doubtless he apprehended that its prevalence would hazard the integrity, if not the very existence, of his own system of religion. For many ages, therefore, it was discountenanced; but, at length, the habit of consulting the stars on important public occasions became frequent, and was attended with as much anxiety and as many absurd ceremonies as disgraced the nations of antiquity. Among the modern Mohammedans, no dignity of state is conferred; no public edifice is founded, except at a time recommended by astrologers. These pretenders to knowledge are supported by persons of rank; and in vain do the more enlightened part of the community exclaim that astrology is a false science. "Do not think," said a prime minister, who had been consulting a soothsayer as to the time of putting on a new dress, " that I am such a fool as to put faith in all this nonsense ;" but I must not make my family unhappy by refusing to comply with forms which some of them deem of consequence."

After these references to the polite literature of the Arabs, it will be expected that they should have paid attention to the natural sciences. They were not, indeed, discoverers and inventors, but they considerably improved upon what they acquired in their extensive intercourse with other nations; and, as forming the link which unites ancient and modern letters, they are entitled to our respect and gratitude. We derive our mathematics from them; and to them, also, we owe much of our astronomical knowledge. Almamoun, by a liberal reward, sought to engage in his service a famous mathematician of Constantinople; and Ibn Korrah enriched the stores of his country in this department with translations of Archimedes and the conics of Apollonius. Some have said that, on the revival of European literature in the fifteenth century, mathematical science was found nearly in the state in which it had been left by Euclid; and the justly celebrated Brücker contends, that the Arabs made no progress whatever in this most important branch of knowledge: later writers, however, and particularly Montucla, the author of the Histoire des Mathematiques, have done ample justice to their researches. Numerical characters, without which our study of the exact sciences were almost in vain, beyond all doubt came to us from the Arabs: not that they invented them —it is probable they were originally words, perhaps Hindu words, expressing the quantities they respectively represent, but abbreviated and brought to their present convenient form by the followers of the Prophet. Trigonometry and algebra are both indebted to their genius. The sines of the one of these sciences instead of the more ancient chord, and the representatives of quantities in the other, descend through the Arabs to us, if they did not at first invent them. Original works on spherical trigonometry are among the productions of Ibn Musa and Geber, the former of whom is accounted the inventor of the solution of equations of the second degree. The University of Leyden still retains a manuscript treatise on the algebra of cubic equations, by Omar ibn Ibrahim; and Casiri, who preserved and classed 1851 manuscripts, even after a fire had destroyed the magnificent collection of the Escurial, informs us, that the principles and praises of algebraic science were sung in an elaborate poem by Alcassem, a native of Grenada.

These departments of knowledge were studied by the Arabs as early as the eighth and ninth centuries.

Astronomy, the science of a pastoral people, and eminently so in regions with an almost cloudless sky, like the East, was studied with great eagerness by Arabian philosophers. Almamoun, who has been before mentioned, was ardently devoted to it: at his cost the necessary instruments of observation were provided, and a complete digest of the science was made. The land where, many ages before, this science had been successfully studied by the Chaldeans, was in his power, and upon its ample plains a degree of the earth's circle was repeatedly measured, so as to determine the whole circumference of the globe to be twenty-four thousand miles. The obliquity of the ecliptic they settled at twenty-three degrees and a half: the annual movement of the equinoxes and the duration of the tropical year were brought to within a very little of the exact observations of modern times, the slight error they admitted resulting from the preference they gave to the system of Ptolemy. Albathani, or, as his name has been Latinized, Albatenius, in the ninth century, after continuing his observations for forty years, drew up tables, known as the Sabean tables, which, though not now in very high repute because of more accurate calculations, were for a long time justly esteemed. Other Arabian astronomers have rendered considerable service to this science. Mohammedanism did not, like ancient paganism, adore the stars; but its disciples studied them with a diligence, without which, perhaps, Newton, Flamstead, and Halley had observed and calculated almost in vain.

Architecture was an art in which the Arabs greatly excelled; their wide extension gave them command of whatever was worthy of observation, and their vast revenues afforded the most abundant means of indulging a taste thus called into exercise. The history of Arabian architecture comprises a period of about eight centuries, including its rise, progress, and decay: their building materials were mostly obtained from the ruined structures and cities that fell into their hands; and if no one particular style was followed by them, it was because they successfully studied most of the styles then known. On their buildings but little external art was bestowed; all their pains were exhausted on the interior, where no expense was spared that could promote luxurious ease and personal comfort. Their walls and ceilings were highly embellished, and the light was mostly admitted in such manner as, by excluding all external objects, to confine the admiration of the spectator to the beauties produced within. With the ar of preserving their structures from decay they must have had an adequate acquaintance. Their stucco composition may still be found as hard as stone, without a crack or flaw : the floors and ceilings of the Alhambra, the ancient palace of Grenada, have been comparatively uninjured by the neglect and dilapidation of nearly seven centuries; while their paint retains its colour so bright and rich as to be occasionally mistaken for mother-of-pearl. Sir Christopher Wren derives the Gothic architecture from the Mohammedans; and the crescent arch, a symbol of one of the deities anciently worshipped throughout the heathen world, was first adopted by the Arabs of Syria, and invariably used in all the edifices erected during the supremacy of the Ommiades. The succeeding dynasty declined following this model; but, during the reign of the house of Moawiyah, in Spain, it was imitated from the Atlantic to the Pyrenees.

The fine arts, painting, and sculpture, were not so much cultivated among the early Mohammedans: they were thought to involve a breach of the divine law. In this particular they agreed with the Jews. Subsequently, however, these scruples were, by degrees, overcome; that style of embellishment denominated Arabesque, which rejects figures of men and animals, being first adopted, and afterward sculpture, more nearly resembling that of modern times. The Alhambra, or palace of that suburb, had its lions, its ornamented tiles, and its paintings. Abdalrahman III. placed a statue of his favourite mistress over the palace he erected for her abode. Music was ardently cultivated. At first, in the desert, its strains were rude and simple; subsequently, the professors of the art were as much cherished, honoured, and rewarded, as were the poets in the courts of the Arab sovereigns. Many were celebrated for their skill in this art, especially Isaac Almouseli. Al Farabi has been denominated the Arabian Orpheus: by his astonishing command of the lute, he could produce laughter, or tears, or sleep in his auditors at pleasure. He wrote a considerable work on music, which is preserved in the Escurial. Abul Faragi is also a famous writer among the Mohammedans on this subject. To them we are indebted for the invention of the lute, which they accounted more perfect than any other instrument; the use, also, of many of our modern instruments, as the organ, flute, harp, tabor, and mandoline, was common among them. Some say that the national instrument of the Scottish highlander is taken from them.

In many of the useful arts of modern days the Arabs were proficients; as agriculture, gardening, metallurgy, and the preparing of leather. The names Morocco and Cordovan are still applied, in this latter art, to leather prepared after the Arabian method. They manufactured and dyed silk and cotton, made paper, were acquainted with the use of gunpowder, and have claims to the honour of inventing the mariner's compass. But perhaps there is no art in which their knowledge is so much a subject of curious inquiry as medicine. Their country was salubrious, their habits simple, and their indulgences few; so that large opportunities of practically studying the art, at least among the Arabs of earlier date, would not occur. Anatomy, except that of the brute creation, was shut up from their study by the prejudices of their creed; yet they excelled in medical skill. Hareth ibn Kaldar, an eminent practitioner settled at Mecca, was honoured with the conversation and applause of Mohammed. Honain was an eminent Arab physician in the middle of the sixth century; Messue, the celebrated preceptor of Almamoun, belonged to this profession; and a host of others adorn the early annals of the Saracens. Al Rhagi, or Rhages, as commonly called, and Abdallah ibn Sina, or Avicenna, are names to which, for centuries, deference was paid by professors of the healing art throughout Europe, though it would not be difficult to show that their doctrines and practice must have been beyond measure absurd. They administered gold, and silver, and precious stones to purify the blood.

Of chymistry, so far as it relates to medicine, the Arabs may be considered as the inventors; and botany, in the same connexion, they cultivated with great success. Geber, in the eighth century, is known as their principal chymical writer; he is said to have composed five hundred volumes, almost every one of which is lost. The early nomenclature of the science indicates how much it owes to this people. Alcohol, alembic, alkali, aludel, and other similar terms, are evidently of Arabic origin; nor should it be forgotten that the characters used for drugs, essences, extracts, and medicines, the import of which is now almost entirely unknown (and which are consequently invested, in vulgar estimation, with occult powers), are all to be traced to the same source.

It may be impossible now to estimate accurately the extent of our obligations to Arabian literature. An empire so widely spread, by the encouragement it gave to letters, must have had a beneficial influence on almost every country. Europeans, whether subject to its sway or only contemplating it from a distance, copied or emulated the example. Gerbert, who subsequently occupied the papal chair as Silvester II., acquired the Arabic method of computation during his travels in Spain, previously to his elevation. Leonardo, a Pisan merchant, obtained a knowledge of the same art in his intercourse with the Mohammedans on the coast of Africa; and by him it was introduced into his own native republic, from whence it was soon communicated to the Western World. In the city of Salernum, a port of Italy, Mussulmans and Christians so intermixed as to communicate insensibly the literature of the Saracens to the Italians, and in the schools of that city students were collected from every quarter of Europe. Arabic books, by command of Charlemagne, were translated into Latin for the use of learned men throughout his vast empire; and, without exaggerating the merits of the followers of the Prophet, it may be admitted that we are indebted to them for the revival of the exact and physical sciences, and for many of those useful arts and inventions that have totally changed the aspect of European literature, and are still contributing to the civilization, freedom, and best interests of man.

X

CHAPTER III.

The present Condition of Mohammedanism.—In Turkey.—The Doctrines believed there.—Their Forms of Devotion.—Lustrations.—Prayer.—Mohammedan Sabbath.—Fast of Ramadan.—Meccan Pilgrimage.—Proselytism.—Mohammedan Hierarchy.—Islamism in Tartary.—In Hindustan.—In China.—In Persia.—In Africa.—In the Indian Archipelago.—The Sooffees.—The Wahabees.

The present condition of the Mohammedan faith, with some account of the standing it maintains in the world, will not be deemed an inappropriate subject for the closing pages of this volume. Its votaries have long ceased to spread alarm through the nations by their victorious and devastating progress; the fire of its fanaticism is almost extinct; nevertheless, its doctrines prevail over a larger number of mankind than any other system of false religion: they are professed in nations and countries remote from each other, and having no other mutual resemblance than that involved in their common superstition. In Spain, indeed, Christianity has triumphed over Islamism; and in the inhospitable regions of Siberia, a part of the ancient Tartary, its advance has been somewhat checked; but in middle and lower Asia, and in Africa, the number of Mohammed's followers has increased. We cannot state with accuracy the number either of Mohammedan or of nominal Christians; but, looking at religion geographically, while Christianity has almost entire dominion in Europe, in Asia Islamism is the dominant faith: in America the cross is rapidly becoming the symbol of faith throughout both its vast continents; but in Africa the crescent waves to the almost entire exclusion of every other emblem.

It is in Turkey that Mohammedanism exists at the present day in its most perfect form. To this country, therefore, our attention shall be first directed.

Constantinople, anciently called Byzantium, and the countries over which the Greek emperors residing in that city reigned, were subdued by the powerful caliphs of Bagdad, while those of Spain and the West were endeavouring to push their conquests over the fairest portions of Europe. The situation of Constantinople and the surrounding empire lay especially open to the Eastern Mohammedans, whose warlike incursions were incessant. Tartars from Asia overran the empire. Othman, in the early part of the thirteenth century, laid the foundation of Turkish greatness. Orchan, Amurath, and Bajazet, his successors, amid both foreign and domestic wars, greatly contributed to its establishment and increase. The children of the last of these conquerors threw the empire into a frightful state of distraction by their unnatural quarrels, till, at last, the youngest of them, named after the Prophet, restored its integrity, and established something like domestic tranquillity. Under a grandson of his, Mohammed II., whom Bayle describes as one of the greatest men recorded in history, the Morea was subjugated, and the Greek empire, so long shaken by internal dissensions, and tottering to dissolution by its luxury, was trampled in the dust by the Moslem conquerors. Constantinople at last yielded to their power, and a palace for the victor was erected on the very spot which Constantine had chosen for his magnificent abode.

From this time to that of Solyman the Magnificent, to whom the Turks owe their laws and police, the empire continued to prosper, but immediately afterward its decline commenced. Letters and science have made but little progress among that people, and their sultans have possessed none of the martial enterprise and energy of their early predecessors; still the faith of Mohammed has maintained, and down to this day continues to maintain, a hold which it enjoys in almost no other country.

The Turks generally repose the most implicit faith in the two leading articles of the Mohammedan creed, that there is but one God, and that Mohammed is his Prophet; and since, in the opinion of the Moslems, a simple assent to these doctrines comprises all that is valuable in religion, and will be surely followed by the possession of heaven, either immediately or remotely, it is readily conceivable that infidelity will be exceedingly rare. In religious matters, the heart opposes not so much what is to be believed as what is to be done.

Minor points of their theology have been from time to time disputed, but these may be regarded as generally settled. Predestination is one of the chief dogmas on which the faith of the Turk is as firmly fixed as on the most momentous article in his creed. Fatalism was the great engine employed by Mohammed in establishing his religion; and among the Turks this doctrine is received as regulating their destiny, controlling all events, and determining the results of every individual's actions; thus unnerving the soul for generous and manly enterprise, and casting a lethargy on the whole nation. In everything the operations of reason are checked, and even made to wait for the imagined manifestations of Deity. According to the creed of the Turks, not only is everything foreknown to God, but everything is predetermined, and brought about by his direct and immediate agency.

The Turk is keen and wise in his ordinary transactions: in promoting his own interests, he knows how to exercise the powers of his mind; but, when difficulty or doubt overtakes him, he makes no effort. The thick cloud of his misfortunes is suffered to remain; his troubles are yielded to with sullen indifference; he considers it impious to oppose the determinations of the Most High. To all improvement, such a doctrine is a decided and invincible foe; in some circumstances, however, it appears to have its advantages. Does a Mohammedan suffer by calamity? Is he plundered or ruined? He does not fruitlessly bewail his lot. His answer to all murmuring suggestions is, "It was written;" and to the most unexpected transition from opulence to poverty, he submits without a sigh. The approach of death does not disturb his tranquillity; he makes his ablution, repeats his prayers, professes his belief in God and his Prophet, and in a last appeal to the aid of affection, he says to his child, " turn my head towards Mecca," and calmly expires.

A people's religion is traced in their established and common forms of devotion, and none are more attentive to these than the Turks. To neglect any ceremony which their religion prescribes, is deemed a mark either of inferior understanding or of depraved character. Public decorum is everywhere observed; and though both moral and religious precepts are violated with impunity and without remorse, they are always spoken of with great respect. A Mohammedan is never ashamed to defend his faith; and of his sincerity and firmness, the earnestness of his vindication may be taken as sufficient proof: he not unfrequently interrupts the progress of conversation by repeating his religious formula. In the Turkish towns, travellers are incessantly met with the cry of Allah Ackbar; and by Mussulmans, who would be esteemed pious, the divine name is as frequently repeated as if reverent and devout thoughts were habitually uppermost in their minds.

Purifications are constantly, and with great strictness, performed by the Mussulmans of every country, but especially by those of Turkey. Their professed object is to render the body fit for the decorous performance of religious duties; no act being praiseworthy or acceptable, in their estimation, unless the person of the performer be in a condition of purity. Some have thought, but without sufficient grounds, that these external purifications are believed to supersede an inward cleansing of the heart. Fountains placed round their mosques, and numerous baths in every city, enable the devout to perform their five prayers daily, during which, if they chance to receive pollution from anything accidentally coming in contact with them, their devotions are suspended till the offensive inconvenience is removed by water or other means.

At the appointed hour, the Maazeens or criers, with their faces towards Mecca, their eyes closed, and their hands upraised, pace the little galleries of the minarets or towers of the mosques, and proclaim in Arabic, the Moslem language of devotion, that the season of prayer has arrived. Instantly, every one, whatever may be his rank or employment, gives himself up to it. Ministers of state suspend the most important affairs, and prostrate themselves on the floor; the tradesman forgets his dealings, and transforms his shop into a place of devotion; and the student lays aside his books, to go through his accustomed supplications. "Never to fail in his prayers" is the highest commendation a Turk can receive; and so prejudicial is the suspicion of irreligion, that even libertines dare not disregard the notices of the Maazeen. The mosques, like chapels in Catholic countries, are always open, and two or three times every day prayers are offered within their walls. It has often been remarked, that the devotions of Christians might acquire something valuable from the gravity, the decorum, and the apparently intense occupation of mind in Turkish worship. The Jews trod their holy place barefoot: the Turks, on the contrary, keep on their boots and shoes. Christians uncover their heads in prayer; the Moslems seldom lay aside their turbans; but for hours they will remain prostrate, or standing in one position, as if absorbed in the most intense abstraction. They have neither altars, pictures, nor statues in their places of worship. Verses of the Koran, the names and personal descriptions of their Prophet, of Ali and his two sons, Hassan and Hosein, with other Moslem saints, are sometimes inscribed in letters of gold on their walls. All distinctions of rank and profession are forgotten when they pray. Persons of every class, on the first sound of the accustomed cry, cast themselves on the ground, and thus declare their belief in the equality of mankind, in the sight of the great Father of all.

The Mohammedans of Turkey have a Sabbath, for which the Jewish or Christian may be supposed to have furnished the model. Friday is their day of rest, which commences on the preceding evening, when the illuminated minarets and colonnades of the mosques give to their cities the appearance of a festival. At noon, on Friday, all business is suspended, the mosques are filled, and prayers are read by the appointed officers, accompanied by the prostrations of the people. Discourses are likewise frequently delivered on practical points in their theology; and sometimes, in the ardour of excitement, political corruption and courtly depravity are fiercely assailed. A voluptuous sultan has been known, under the effect of these discourses, to tear himself from the soft indulgences of his harem and court, to lead his martial subjects to war and victory on the plains of their enemies. As soon as the public religious services are concluded, all return to their ordinary pursuits; the day, however, is strictly observed by all classes in the manner prescribed by law, it being a received maxim that he who, without legitimate cause, absents himself from public devotion on three successive Fridays, abjures his religion. It is worthy of observation, that the prayers of the Turks consist chiefly of adoration, of confessions of the Divine attributes and the nothingness of man, and of homage and gratitude to the Supreme Being. A Turk must not pray for the frail and perishable blessings of this life; the health of the sultan, the prosperity of his country, and divisions and wars among the Christians alone excepted. The legitimate object of prayer they hold to be spiritual gifts, and happiness in a future state of being.

No one of their religious institutions is more strictly observed by the Turks than the fast of Ramadan. He who violates it is reckoned either an infidel or an apostate; and if two witnesses establish his offence, he is deemed to have incurred the severest penalty of the law. Abstinence from food, and even from the use of perfumes, from sunrise to sunset, is enjoined. The rich pass the hours in meditation and prayer, tne grandees sleep away their time, but the labouring man, pursuing his daily toil, most heavily feels its rigour. " When the month of Ramadan happens in the extremities of the seasons, the prescribed abstinence is almost intolerable, and is more severe than the practice of any moral duty, even to the most vicious and depraved of mankind." During the day all traffic is suspended; but in the evening, and till late at night, it is actively carried on in the streets, shops, and bazars, most splendidly illuminated. From sunset to sunrise, revelry and excess are indulged in. Every night there is a feast among the great officers of the court: the reserve of the Turkish character is laid aside, and friends and relations cement their union by mutual intercourse. Sumptuous banquets and convivial hilarity are universal; and, were not women everywhere excluded from the tables of the men, the pleasure of the festivals would amply compensate the rigorous self-denial of their fasts.

The pilgrimage to Mecca is with the Turks more a matter of form than of reality. Its importance as a part of the Moslem ritual is admitted, and apparently felt, but the number of pilgrims annually decreases. The sultan, having dominion over the country through which the pilgrims must pass, preserves the public ways leading to the venerated city; the best soldiers of his empire are charged with the protection of the caravans, which are sometimes numerous; but of his own subjects, properly so called, few comparatively accompany them; they are made up of devotees from a greater distance. The sultan, no doubt, encourages the pilgrimage as much on commercial as on religious grounds. The Koran has determined it to be very proper to intermingle commerce and religion: "It shall be no crime in you," it says, "if ye seek an increase from your Lord by trading during the pilgrimage." Accordingly, articles of easy carriage and ready sale are brought by the pilgrims from every country. The productions and manufactures of India thus find their way into other parts of Asia and throughout Africa. The muslins and chintses of Bengal and the Deccan, the shawls of Cashmere, the pepper of Malabar, the diamonds of Golconda, the pearls of Kilkau, the cinnamon of Ceylon, and the spices of the Moluccas, are made to yield advantage to the Ottoman empire, and the luxury of its subjects is sustained by contributions from the most distant nations.

Mohammedans of the present day, at least those of Turkey, are less anxious to make proselytes than were those of a former age. Those of India and Africa may, to some extent, still retain the sentiment, that to convert infidels is an ordinance of God, and must be observed by the faithful in all ages; but in Turkey little desire of this kind is felt, chiefly because, by a refinement of uncharitableness, the conversion of the world is deemed unworthy of their endeavours. Now and then a devout Moslem, instigated by zeal or personal attachment, may offer up this prayer for a Jew or a Christian: " Great God, enlighten this infidel, and graciously dispose his heart to embrace thy holy religion;" and perhaps to a youth, esteemed for his talents or knowledge, the language of persuasion may occasionally be addressed with an air of gentleness and urbanity; but the zeal of the missionary is in such cases commonly subject to what are conceived to be the rules of good breeding, and a vague reply or silence is regarded as an indication that the subject is disagreeable, and should not be continued. A Mussulman may pray for the conversion of infidels, but, till they are converted, no blessing may be supplicated in their behalf. "Their death is eternal, why pray for them?" is the language of the Mohammedan creed: do not "defile your feet by passing over the graves of men who are enemies of God and of his Prophet."

Of the Mohammedan hierarchy, some idea may be obtained from the form it assumes in Turkey. The Koran is considered the treasure of all laws, divine and human, and the caliphs as the depositaries of this treasure; so that they are at once the pontiffs, legislators, and judges of the people, and their office combines all authority, whether sacerdotal, regal, or judicial. To the grand sultan titles are given, styling him the vicar, or the shadow of God. The several powers which pertain to him in this august capacity are delegated to a body of learned men, called the Oulema. In this body three descriptions of officers are included: the ministers of religion, called the Imams; the expounders of the law, called the Muftis; and the ministers of justice, called the Cadis. The ministers of religion are divided into chief and inferior, the former of whom only belong to the Oulema. Both classes are made up of Sheiks, or ordinary preachers; the Khatibs, readers or deacons; the Imams, a title comprising those who perform the service of the mosque on ordinary days, and those to whom pertain the ceremonies of circumcision, marriage, and burial; the Maazeens, or criers, who announce the hours of prayer; and the Cayuns, or common attendants of the mosque. The idea of this classification was, perhaps, taken from the Mosaic priesthood; the Khatib being the Aaron, and the next four the several orders of the Levites, with their servants or helpers. The imperial temples have one Sheik, one Khatib, from two to four Imams, twelve Maazeens, and twenty Cayuns, among whom, except in a few of the chief mosques of Constantinople, the Khatibs have the pre-eminence. All these ministers are subject to the civil magistrate, who is looked upon as a sort of diocesan, and who may perform at any time all the sacerdotal functions. The ministers of religion are not distinguishable from other people; they mix in the same society, engage in similar pursuits, and affect no greater austerity than marks the behaviour of Mussulmans generally. Their influence depends entirely on their reputation for learning and talents, for gravity and correct moral conduct; their employment is, for the most part, very simple, as chanting aloud the public service, and performing such offices as every master of a family may discharge. As Mohammedanism acknowledges no sacrifices, it appoints no priests; the duties performed by the ministers of religion being seemingly devolved on them more as a matter of convenience than on account of any sacredness attaching to their order.

The vast country to which the general name of

Tartary has been given, is that from whence Mohammedanism has gone forth to the East, the West, and the South. In Thibet, the Grand Lama and various national idols hold divided empire with the Prophet; and in the inhospitable regions of Siberia, the churches of Greece and Russia have successfully promulgated the Christian doctrines; while the Circassians, with some other Tartar races, are almost without religion. In the Crimea, the people are Mussulmans, as rigid and devoted as the Turks; and over the vast tract called by modern geographers Independent Tartary, the crescent triumphantly waves. From these regions sprung, in the earlier ages of Mohammedan conquest, those vast empires which, in the East, comprise so large a number of the professors of the faith of Islam. The first sovereign of this country, to whom the title of sultan was awarded early in the tenth century, conducted several expeditions into Hindustan, and secured the homage of many of the cities. The ancient Indian superstition was in a great measure overturned by his victorious arms. Long and fierce contests ensued: the princes of the subdued provinces, often throwing off their forced allegiance, endeavoured to regain their independence and re-establish their ancient faith, till, at length, the great Timurlane, having overrun the country with his legions, received at Agra the title of Emperor of Hindustan. Scarcely, however, had two centuries and a half rolled away, when his successors fell in their turn under the Persian power; and the empire he established was weakened, and ultimately destroyed. As the result of these conquests, Mohammedanism prevailed to a great extent, but rather nominally than really, among the millions of India: it was the religion of the court and government; but, either from indifference or timidity in the Moslem conquerors, the ancient idols still held extensive influence, and were at length gradually restored. In the twelfth century, Benares, the ancient seat of Brahminical learning and of Hindu idolatry, fell into the hands of the conqueror, who destroyed its numerous objects of popular adoration. Yet, soon afterward, the religious character of the place was restored, and the demolished idols were replaced by others, that were as eagerly resorted to as had been their predecessors. To this consecrated metropolis, a pilgrimage was regarded by the millions of India as imperatively commanded, and as necessary as was a visit to Mecca by the Mohammedans; and the weakness or the policy of its Moslem conquerors did not long withhold from them this valued privilege; the government of the city was committed to the Hindus, and their conquerors, in the plenitude of their bigotry, pride, and power, never thought of suffering their own magistrates to exercise authority within its walls. Thus Mohammedanism is the religion, not of the ancient inhabitants of India, but of the descendants of the millions of Tartars, Persians, and Arabians who, at various periods, have left their native seats to participate in the riches of these far-famed plains. The north and northwestern parts are filled with them, and from thence they have wandered over the whole of that vast country. Perhaps their numbers may now amount to nearly twenty millions, among whom, however, though they are mostly of foreign extraction, are many converts from Hinduism. They form separate communities, amalgamating in some parts of the country, and living as sociably with Hindus as the differences in their respective faiths will permit. Hindu princes have at times paid their devotions at Mohammedan shrines, and observed their feasts; while Mohammedans have relaxed somewhat the strictness of their observances, and manifested an inclination to conform, as far as possible, to their Hindu neighbours. Some five centuries ago, the Borahs, a people who once occupied the kingdom of Guzerat, were converted *en masse* to Islamism. The Arab traders to the coasts of Malabar have always been exceedingly earnest in their endeavours to convert the natives, in which they have been greatly aided by the facility with which they have been allowed to purchase the children of the poorer classes, to educate them in the principles of their faith, and also by the frequency with which the inhabitants of those districts lose caste. This badge of the Hindu faith is often forfeited by the people mixing with those of other countries, and when it is lost they easily become Moslems.

It has been maintained that the native inhabitants of India are absolutely unchangeable in their sacred, domestic, and political institutions, and, at first sight, there would appear to be much to warrant such an opinion; but the history of many of them, and especially of the Sikhs, who inhabit the provinces of the Panjab, between the rivers Jumna and Indus, may be alleged as proofs to the contrary. Still, in the religion of the Sikhs, Mohammedan fable and Hindu absurdity are mixed; its founder wishing to unite both these prevalent systems in one. He had been educated in a part of the country where these two religions appeared to touch each other, if not commingle, and he was no stranger to the violent animosity existing between their respective professors; he sought, therefore, to blend the jarring elements of both in peaceful union. The Hindu was required to abandon his idols, and to worship the one Supreme Deity whom his religion acknowledged; while the Mohammedan was to abstain from such practices (especially the killing of cows) as were offensive to the superstition of the Hindus. This plan so far prevailed, that, without acknowledging the Prophet, the Sikhs became more Mohammedans than Hindus; and though the institutions of Brahma are not admitted among them, they insult and persecute true Moslems more fiercely and cruelly than any other people. They compel them to eat that which is forbidden by their law; animals which they account unclean are frequently thrown into their places of public assembly, and they are prohibited from proclaiming the hour of prayer to the faithful.

China is one of those countries to which Mohammedanism was carried by the hordes of Tartary. From the scrupulous jealousy with which this vast empire is guarded from observation, it is difficult to say to what extent the Mohammedan faith, or, indeed, any other, prevails among its numberless inhabitants; but, beyond question, it is tolerated.

The irruption of the Saracens into China under Walid can scarcely be termed a conquest. Subsequently, the successors of Zenghis Khan seated themselves on the throne of Pekin, and opened the country to an intercourse with all nations. The commercial Arabs had visited the ports and cities in the south of China; and, now that access to the apital was unrestrained, multitudes of them repaired thither. They acquired the language, and adopted the dress and manners of the people, to whom also they rendered valuable aid in adjusting their chronology, and making the necessary calculations for their calendar. Intercourse with the Chinese made the Mohammedans desirous of effecting their conversion, the means adopted for which were both wise and humane. Deserted children were taken under their protection, and educated in Islamism; while in other ways they sought to commend themselves to confidence, and their religion to respect, by alleviating the wretchedness induced by a cruel superstition. The Mohammedans of China seem to partake of the mild and quiet character of the inhabitants generally, and are therefore tolerated; though there have been some exceptions to this encomium. About sixty years ago they were instrumental in promoting an unsuccessful rebellion, and the Emperor Kien Long, after suppressing it, ordered one hundred thousand of them to be put to death.

Persia, from an early period, has been almost entirely a Mohammedan country. On its conquest by the Saracens, the religion of Zoroaster, which had till then prevailed, was nearly abolished. Those who persevered in retaining it were obliged to flee to the mountains or to the western parts of India, where their old forms of worship still linger. In the disputes which ensued on the death of Mohammed concerning the caliphate, the Persians espoused the cause of Ali, the Prophet's son-in-law, and to his memory they are still attached. "May this arrow go to the heart of Omar," is a frequent expression among them in drawing a bow; and not long since, when Mr. Malcolm, during his travels in Persia, was praising Omar, the antagonist of Ali, as the greatest of the caliphs, a Persian, overcome by the justice of his observations, yet still adhering to his rooted prejudices, replied, "This is all very true, but he was a dog after all."

Here Mohammedanism exists in a less rigorous form than in Turkey. Its ceremonies are observed by those who are little disposed to practice its moral code: they say their prayers at the appointed season, and make a show of devotion to prevent their being suspected of irreligion; but the people generally are little concerned about the pilgrimage to Mecca, and other matters on which, in the Koran, much stress is laid. They choose rather to resort to the tomb of Ali, and to that of his son Hosein, whose name is reverenced among them with a feeling approaching to adoration.

In Africa, Mohammedanism has very widely prevailed. Algiers, Tunis, Tripoli, all the northern parts of this continent, acknowledge its sway.

From Arabia and Egypt it spread west and south nearly to the great rivers. It is the established religion of Morocco; and in Western Barbary and several kingdoms of the interior the Arabic language is spoken, the Koran believed, and the Prophet almost worshipped. The Senegal, up to the small Moorish state of Gedumah, is the line of division between the Mohammedans and the Negroes: from thence the line passes eastward of north, through Nigritia and Nubia to the Nile. As yet, however, it is but indistinctly marked, it being doubtful whether Timbuctoo is a Mohammedan or Negro town. The courts of Bornou and Cassina are Mohammedan, but a majority of their subjects are pagans. Islamism in these vast territories is in an exceedingly degenerate state when compared with either its first development in the Arabian desert, or with what now obtains in Turkey. It is said that but little more than its exclusive persecuting spirit remains: the Oriental lustrations are almost unknown, Mohammedan temperance is neglected, and the great doctrine of the unity of God is confounded with, or supplanted by, the polytheism of the native inhabitants. The Mussulman is more depraved than the pagan; so that, while travellers frequently mention the hospitality they received from the latter, by the former they were constantly insulted and annoyed on account of their religion. In no quarter of the world does the faith of the Prophet wear so frightful an aspect as in Africa.

The region from which Mohammedanism first sprung has not remained in all respects faithful to the precepts of the Prophet. In Mecca and Medina, indeed, his name and system are held in the profoundest veneration; and no wonder, since both these cities are mainly supported by the superstitious observances enjoined in the Koran; but the Bedouins are as licentious in their religion as in their policy and habits. On the Turkish frontiers they keep up an appearance of respect for the name of the Prophet and his doctrines; but, in answer to all reproaches for their unfaithfulness, they say in words worthy a better taught and more civilized race, "The religion of Mohammed could never have been intended for us. We have no water in the desert. How, then, can we make the prescribed ablutions? We have no money. How, then, can we give alms? The fast of Ramadan is a useless command to persons who fast all the year round; and, if God be everywhere, why should we go to Mecca to adore him?"

From the southernmost part of Hindustan, Mohammedanism made its way to the Malayan peninsula; to Sumatra, Java, Borneo, the Manillas, and the Celebes: Goram, one of the Spice Islands, is its eastern boundary. In the interior of these islands it prevails less than on the shores. To these remote regions Islamism has been carried more by the commercial than the military enterprise of its votaries. What is its present condition there, it is difficult, perhaps impossible, accurately to ascertain. In Java it was the established religion; but, when the Dutch settled that island early in the seventeenth century, many of the natives were converted. Little respect is paid by the Javans of the present day either to their ancient paganism, or to Mohammedanism which took its place; though some of the forms of the latter are still in force, and its institutions are said to be gaining ground.

The reader of Mohammedan history will meet with the terms Sooffee and Wahabee, as designating certain divisions of the disciples of the religion of the Prophet. It will not, therefore, be inappropriate to close with a brief account of these respective sects.

Sooffee is a term originating in Persia, meaning enthusiasts or mystics, or persons distinguished by extraordinary sanctity. The object of the Sooffee is to attain a divine beatitude, which he describes as consisting in absorption into the essence of Deity. The soul, according to his doctrine, is an emanation from God, partaking of his nature; just as the rays of light are emanations from the sun, and of the same nature with the source from whence they are derived. The creature and the Creator are of one substance. No one can become a Sooffee without strictly conforming to the established religion, and practising every social virtue; and when, by this means, he has gained a habit of devotion, he may exchange what they style practical for spiritual worship, and abandon the observance of all religious forms and ceremonies. He at length becomes inspired, arrives at truth, drops his corporeal veil, and mixes again with that glorious essence from which he has been partially and for a time separated. The life of the Sooffees of Persia, though generally austere, is not rendered miserable, like that of the visionary devotees of Hinduism, by the practice of dreadful severities, their most celebrated teachers have been famed for knowledge and devotion. The Persians are a poetic people, and the very genius of Sooffeeism is poetry. Its raptures are the raptures of inspiration; its hopes are those of a highly sensitive and excited imagination; its writers in the sweetest strains celebrate the Divine love, which pervades all nature: everything, from the very highest to the lowest, seeking and tending towards union with Deity as its object of supreme desire. They inculcate forbearance, abstemiousness, and universal benevolence. They are unqualified predestinarians. The emanating principle, or the soul, proceeding from God, can do nothing, they say, without his will, nor refuse to do anything which he instigates. Some of them, consequently, deny the existence of evil; and the doctrine of rewards and punishments is superseded by their idea of re-absorption into the Divine essence. The free opinions of this class of enthusiasts subvert the doctrines of Islamism, yet they pay an outward respect to them; they unsettle the existing belief, without providing an intelligible substitute; they admit the divine mission of the Prophet, but explain away the dogmas he uttered· and while they affect to yield him honour as a person raised up by God, to induce moral order in the world, they boast their own direct and familiar intercourse with Deity, and claim, on that account, unqualified obedience in all that relates to spiritual interests.

The similarity of Sooffeeism to the ancient Pythagorean and Platonic doctrines will occur to every one at all acquainted with the religion and philosophy of antiquity. It as closely resembles some of the distinguishing tenets of the Brahminical faith. In fact, it seems as if designed, in conjunction with the refined theology of ancient, and the sublime visions of modern idolators, to teach us that, without Divine guidance, the loftiest human conceptions on subjects connected with God and religion invariably err; the ignorant and the instructed are equally wrong; "the world by wisdom knows not God."

The Wahabees are a modern sect of Mohammedan reformers, whose efforts have considerably changed the aspect of the religion of the Prophet. Perhaps to them may be owing much of that rigid adherence to Mohammedan doctrine and practice which prevails in those parts where their influence has been felt. They are the followers of Abdol Wahab, who commenced his career in the region where, during the lifetime of the Prophet, Moseilama had threatened a considerable division among his followers. Wahab was an ambitious fanatic, who aimed, nevertheless, at reforming the national religion. He was aided by powerful princes of the province of Nejed; and, within a short time, the tenets he maintained spread throughout the peninsula. His fundamental principle, like that of Mohammed, was the unity of God. The Koran he regarded as divine, rejecting all the glosses which ignorance and infatuation had put upon it, and holding in utter contempt all the traditions and tales concerning its author, which the devout of every generation had eagerly received. The reverence, approaching to adoration, which the Arabs were wont to pay to the name of Mohammed, all visits to his tomb, and all regard to the tombs and relics of Arab saints, he denounced; and the costly ornaments with which a mistaken piety had enriched these sacred spots, he thought might be appropriated to ordinary purposes. Wahab would not suffer the common oath of, by Mohammed, or by Ali, to be used among his followers, on the very rational ground that an oath is an appeal to a witness of our secret thoughts, and who can know these but God? The title of Lord, generally given to the Prophet by his followers, Wahab rejected as impious. He was commonly mentioned by this zealous reformer and his adherents by his simple name, without the addition of " our Lord, the Prophet of God." All who deviated in any degree from the plain sense of the Koran, either in belief or practice, were infidels in their esteem; upon whom, therefore, according to its directions, war might be made. Thus was the martial spirit of the early Saracens again called into exercise; and with the ardour that characterized the days of the immediate successors of the Prophet, they were prepared at once to assail the consciences and the property of men not exactly of their own faith.

At the call of their leader, they assembled first in the plain of Draaiya, some 400 miles east of Medina, armed and provided at their own expense for war. Bagdad and Mecca in vain attempted to suppress them; the seraglio itself was filled with their formidable war-cry; the sultan trembled on his throne; and the caravans from Syria suspended their usual journeys. The imperial city suffered from their ravages in its usual supplies of coffee; and the terror of their name was widely spreading among devout Mohammedans of every country, for they had violated the shrines of saints, and levelled to the ground the chapels at Mecca, which devotion had consecrated to the memory of the Prophet and his family. At the commencement of the present century, however, Mecca was recovered from them by the Turkish arms, and the plague, with the smallpox, breaking out just at this time among the followers of Wahab, probably saved the mighty fabric of Islamism. These reverses did not quench, however, the ardour of the Wahabees. Their leader had been assassinated, but his son, already distinguished for his prudence and valour, succeeded him in the command. Medina fell beneath his power, and from thence to the Persian Gulf he seemed likely to reign lord paramount. In 1805 he was able to impose a heavy tax on the caravan of pilgrims from Damascus to the Holy City, and declared that thenceforth it should consist of pilgrims alone, without the pride and pomp of a religious procession. Soon afterward they again entered Mecca, and immediately threatened with destruction every sacred relic; but they did not put their threats into execution. Various conflicts between them and the orthodox Mohammedans have since ensued, the general result of which has been to break the martial and fanatical spirit of the Wahabees, and to re-establish the power of the grand sultan in cities and districts where it had been placed in jeopardy. They are still, indeed, dreaded as plunderers, but no great national convulsion has resulted from their efforts.

Some writers regret the suppression of this once powerful sect of Mohammedans, believing that, if continued, they would have been instrumental in overthrowing the Moslem faith, and making way for a purer religion; but for ourselves, we see little occasion for these regrets. The Wahabees must not be supposed more favourable to a pure faith than are those by whom they have been overthrown. If they must be regarded as reformers, they only attempted to correct a few absurd and scandalous practices: the impious and abominable dogmas of the Koran they left untouched; or, if they touched them, it was only to enforce their observance with greater rigour. Their creed was even more sanguinary and intolerant than that of the ancient Mohammedans, and probably the continuance of their power would have been nothing more than the continuance of injustice, cruelty, and persecution. We do not look for the overthrow of Mohammedanism by such means. One system of error may sometimes destroy another, but the pure faith, which blesses a miserable world by directing men in the path of safety, knowledge, and happiness, will extend only as the sacred volume is diffused, and as that holy influence from God accompanies it by which the understanding is illuminated and the heart renewed. Fanaticism is no auxiliary of the religion of the Bible; it neither prepares its way nor accelerates its progress. Violence and war are utterly rejected by this divine system, as alien from its spirit and character. "My kingdom," says its founder, "is not of this world: if my kingdom were of this world, then would my servants fight; but now is my kingdom not from hence."

THE END.

www.ingramcontent.com/pod-product-compliance
Lightning Source LLC
Chambersburg PA
CBHW032055220426
43664CB00008B/1007